creative
neighbourhoods

"You can always learn no matter what age – up 'til the project I didn't even know how to take a photograph."

Mary Hayes, participant, Tenants in Focus

creative
neighbourhoods

the role of the arts in building
sustainable communities

Graeme Beedham BA (Hons) MA FCIH

Alvin Wade FCIH

Aston Housing Consultancy

contents

jon rouse
chief executive, housing corporation

When we launched the 'Involvement Policy for the Housing Association Sector' in 2003, we said that we expect all housing associations to clearly show how their services have been commented on and influenced by the people living in their homes. We also expected housing associations to be able to show that responding to residents' views is something that runs through all their activities as part of their culture and the way they deliver services, and equally as important, we expect them to work alongside residents to decide the best ways of involving them depending on their circumstances. Involving residents is an essential ingredient of a quality housing service, especially as part of continuous improvement.

One key aspect of housing association business is regeneration of communities. One of the outcomes of our regeneration and market renewal policy, *Adding Value To What We Have*, launched in 2004 is: *'there is a resident and customer centred approach, with high levels of involvement to assist in* *making the regeneration sustainable and 'owned' by the community.'*

While we expect all associations to have involvement as a central part of their business, how each association, and their residents achieve this must suit their circumstances. Therefore we welcome the publication of the handbook *'Creative Neighbourhoods: the role of the arts in building sustainable communities'* which offers some practical and innovative solutions, and good practice guidance for housing associations and residents groups alike.

Positive proof that the use of the arts as a practical and meaningful way for associations and residents to effectively expand their confidence and influence with each other is certainly another technique to explore.

6

peter hewitt
chief executive,
arts council england

The Arts Council believes that the arts have the power to transform lives and communities. *Creative Neighbourhoods* illustrates just how effectively they can do this when embedded within housing and regeneration programmes. It draws together a selection from the growing number of imaginative arts projects that have been led by housing associations and residents' groups across England and Wales. In doing so, it reminds us that bricks and mortar alone cannot create a sense of community. Design quality and the physical environment are key factors. But equally important are the interactions between people, their attitudes, and the kinds of activities and opportunities provided in a locality.

There is huge appetite for the arts across the country. Our report, *Arts in England*, found that 87% of the population had participated in at least one arts activity in the last year. However, there can be many barriers to access and participation. Not everyone has the option of travelling regularly to venues outside their local area, particularly the young, those with disabilities, the elderly and the disadvantaged.

The case studies in *Creative Neighbourhoods* are all about local provision, about bringing the arts into the heart of communities. Some involve professional artists working with residents and architects on major refurbishment schemes. Others are about the development of new community spaces and resources for creative activities. All appear to demonstrate the role of the arts in improving consultation and communication with residents, a role that can be vitally important during times of major change and regeneration. Equally evident are the more personal and social impacts of these arts projects, the ways in which they have transformed individual lives, helped bind communities more closely together, and create a real sense of local pride and identity. For this reason, I believe that *Creative Neighbourhoods* will offer both inspiration and practical guidance to anyone with an interest in housing, regeneration, and how to build vibrant and sustainable communities in the future.

7

introduction

this good practice guide aims
to demonstrate:

- how support for community arts
  projects can help the housing sector,
  particularly housing associations; to
  increase resident involvement
- how arts projects can contribute to the
  regeneration of declining communities
- how arts projects are a valid use of
  scarce resources
- how housing associations, community
  groups and individuals can access
  funding to support arts initiatives

While social landlords have come to recognise the value of resident participation, achieving it can create new demands on all involved.

10

The guide draws together case studies from a range of arts projects commissioned by residents or housing providers over the last few years in England and Wales. It considers how the arts has been embedded into wider housing development and refurbishment programmes, and its role in contributing to these programmes, increasing social capital and tackling exclusion.

The first section presents an overview of existing research and evaluation studies into the social impact of community-based arts projects, and some of their measurable outcomes in terms of social inclusion, education, health, crime reduction and quality of life. It looks at evidence of how arts projects can contribute to the image and liveability of neighbourhoods, and can increase levels of resident participation in local decision-making and consultation.

The second section provides more detailed descriptions of selected case studies. Through interviews with participants, it explores the contribution of arts initiatives to the physical and economic aspects of regeneration and also to its social dimension – exploring how different projects have impacted on individuals and helped create a sense of community, networks, reciprocity and confidence.

The final section offers practical guidance to housing managers, organisations and resident groups who are interested in developing their own arts programmes and initiatives. It provides advice on planning a suitable arts project for an area or neighbourhood, engaging the community, selecting artists and accessing funding.

Why is resident participation important?

Resident participation is considered important for the following reasons:

- residents deserve a real say in what is happening to them, their homes and their communities
- residents have knowledge about their homes and communities that their landlords dont have
- partnership and consultation with residents helps housing organisations to make better decisions, improve services and avoid the mistakes of the past
- resident participation harnesses resources to benefit both landlord and residents
- resident participation tends to make people more positive about any change process and its outcomes

While social landlords have come to recognise the value of resident participation, achieving it can create new demands on all involved. Residents might be invited to participate in regeneration partnerships, social housing governance structures, best value review groups, customer panels, service level inspection groups, and as tenant inspectors to name a few. Attracting, motivating and sustaining the active engagement of residents through these mechanisms can be difficult and time-consuming. The cultural diversity of many communities can also pose challenges,

... different projects have impacted on individuals and helped create a sense of community, networks, reciprocity and confidence.

11

with minority groups often less responsive to traditional methods of engagement. New tools and methods have been tried, such as resident participation compacts or payment for residents to attend meetings and sit on boards. However, all too often participation becomes dependent upon a potentially unrepresentative few, or participatory goodwill becomes exhausted and levels of engagement collapse. A common complaint from community representatives is that they feel standard models of resident participation are simply being imposed on them, rather than tailored to the specific needs of their communities.

Housing associations are increasingly seeing themselves not simply as housing providers, but also as regeneration agencies. As such, they have a role to play in tackling the social exclusion experienced by many of their residents living in some of the most deprived wards in the country. The governments Sustainable Communities Plan makes clear that top down regeneration doesn't work. Housing associations will only be successful in contributing to regeneration objectives if they work in partnership with local residents. However, problems can be compounded in the most deprived communities by a sense of powerlessness and abandonment, and by the need to strengthen community networks and organisations before resident consultation can even begin.

In this context, many housing associations are beginning to look beyond formal mechanisms and exploring more imaginative ways of involving residents in local regeneration initiatives. Arts activities are being used to open up new ways of communicating – through music, performance, narrative and the visual arts – which have a relevance to local people. Such approaches can offer a relatively cost-effective, non-confrontational way to increase participation, enhance community spirit, reduce crime and improve landlord-tenant relationships. They have also been shown to be a particularly effective way of engaging previously excluded groups in decision-making processes.

The nature and variety of arts activities means that their effect on a community can often be far-reaching and very apparent to those who are directly involved, but difficult to measure quantitatively.

Evidence of the impact of the arts

"Participation in cultural activities can and does deliver a sense of belonging, trust and civic engagement [and] can not only lead to social regeneration but can be a catayst for crime reduction and learning."
Culture at the Heart of Regeneration (DCMS June 2004)

"I am convinced of the part that culture plays in the regeneration of neighbourhoods, deprived areas and entire cities. We have seen the effect of great flagship buildings and public art throughout the country, but can now also reap the benefit at community level of local cultural initiatives."
The Rt Hon Tessa Jowell MP, Secretary of State for Culture, Media and Sport, in her foreword to *Releasing Potential, Creativity and Change – Arts and Regeneration in Englands North West.* (Moriarty and McManus 2003)

The section aims to summarise some of the findings of recent research into the impact of community-based arts projects. The nature and variety of arts activities means that their effect on a community can often be far-reaching and very apparent to those who are directly involved, but difficult to measure quantitatively. Capturing outcomes in terms of individual lives or social networks generally requires more in-depth, qualitative evaluation, or personal testimonies like those reported in the case studies later in this guide.

However, there have been a significant number of studies published around the world in recent years which have aimed to provide a more rigorous evaluation of the contribution of arts activities to social inclusion, health, education and community cohesion outcomes. While it is not possible to discuss these publications in depth here, we have drawn together some of the conclusions and evidence from key studies in this field, and sign-posted to further reading. The focus is on those outcomes of greatest interest to the housing sector – social inclusion and community cohesion, skills and employment, and crime reduction.

Arts activities are being used to open up new ways of communicating – through music, performance, narrative and the visual arts – which have a relevance to local people.

Social inclusion

The Social Exclusion Unit's September 1998 report on neighbourhood renewal argued that renewal programmes were less effective when imposed from above, with little involvement of the community they are supposed to benefit. Policy Action Team 10 (PAT 10) was one of a number of action teams set up in the wake of the Social Exclusion Unit's report to collect further evidence about what worked best. PAT 10 aimed to establish whether arts, sport and leisure could be used as a tool to engage people and support social inclusion, particularly in disadvantaged neighbourhoods. The PAT 10 report concluded that the arts and sport:

- lend themselves naturally to voluntary collaborative arrangements which help develop a sense of community
- help communities to express their identity and develop their own self-reliant organisations
- are activities in which people participate willingly, and in which there is widespread interest, including from young people at risk of social exclusion
- give individuals social, organisational and marketable skills
- can communicate directly with individuals and groups and bring out hidden talents which have a lasting effect on the persons life
- give individuals a greater sense of achievement, self-respect and self-confidence (DCMS 1999: 30/31)

Similarly, Policy Action Team 9's report, *Community Self-Help* reported on the role of the arts in building sustainable communities, describing how participatory arts projects, such as festivals, murals and drama can act as a starting point for more organised community involvement. (Home Office, 1999: 5)

13

Over 60 of the residents directly participated in the project in different ways, including visiting galleries, selecting the artists, organising private views, and hosting events in the blocks. Many more residents went along to see the work. The Housing Action Trust were impressed with the outcomes ...

Further up in the air, sheil park, liverpool

For a month at a time, six different artists would live in the tower block ...

In the five years since the Policy Action Team reports were published, a growing body of evidence about the value of the arts in addressing social exclusion has emerged – much of this listed in the bibliography. At the forefront of this work have been organisations such as Arts Council England and Comedia, and further lists of relevant publications are available on both of these organisations websites. The table below summarises some of the more detailed studies and their findings.

Study and Methodology Impacts

Use or Ornament? The Social Impact of Participation in the Arts (Matarasso, F., Comedia 1997)
Method: case study research in nine UK locations, Helsinki and New York; project visits, formal interviews and focus group discussions. Presents evidence that the arts:

The role of the arts in building confidence, motivation and self-esteem also emerges as an important factor in creating routes through to further education and employment.

- improve social cohesion
- support community empowerment and self-determination
- enhance local image and identity
- contribute to personal development, imagination and vision
- improve health and well being

How the Arts Measure up: The Social Impact of the Arts (Williams, D., Comedia 1997)
Method: two-year Australian study focused on measuring the impact of 95 community based arts projects; nine case studies; survey of 198 organisers and 200 observers. Indicators developed to assess the social, artistic, economic and educational benefits of the projects. Presents evidence that the arts:

- develop social capital
- build and develop community cohesion
- activate social change
- improve economic performance

Policy Action Team 10 Report and The Arts and Neighbourhood Renewal – a literature review to inform the work of Policy Action Team 10 (DCMS and Shaw 1999)
Method: meetings between officials and practitioners; subgroups on specific issues (best practice, funding, etc); submissions from organisations; visits to six arts agencies; literature review of existing research. Presents evidence that the arts:

- develop self-confidence, self-respect and a sense of achievement
- increase social, organisational and marketable skills
- produce economic benefits
- help communities express their identity

- change perceptions of neighbourhoods
- build outside links for insular communities
- increase employability

The Role of the Arts in Regeneration (Blake Stevenson Ltd, Scottish Executive Central Research Unit, 2000)
Method: extensive literature review and four case studies .Presents evidence that the arts:

- improve an areas image
- attract economic investment
- support community development
- lead to training and employment
- support individuals personal development
- help engage hard to reach people in regeneration programmes

Releasing the Potential: Creativity and Change (Moriarty, G, McManus K, Arts Council England 2003)
Method: fifteen case studies of community arts projects in the North West of England, focusing on their role in bringing social cohesion, prosperity and employment to areas where traditional industries have declined. Presents evidence that the arts:

- interrupt negative and disruptive patterns
- build confidence and self esteem
- develop self discipline
- offer relatively neutral territory within which those from different backgrounds can explore diversity and commonality

The types of skills fostered by arts activities are increasingly relevant in todays jobs market.

17

Skills and employment

Many of the studies and evaluations of arts projects in community settings, including those summarised above, have demonstrated successful outcomes in relation to the skills and employability of participants. Providing creative learning opportunities at a local level also appears to offer an effective route into further training or employment, particularly for young people at risk of exclusion.

Since the *All Our Futures* report by the National Advisory Committee of Creative and Cultural Education (NACCE) in 1999, there has also been a growing body of evidence from educational research, which examines the impact of the arts and creativity on learning. The report by Anna Craft for the Qualifications and Curriculum Authority in 2001 provides a fairly comprehensive analysis of research and literature on creativity in education. While tending to focus on arts provision in more formal education settings, this research is relevant in showing how creative activities help develop the more transferable skills sought after by most

Many participants have gone on to access further learning, education or employment as a direct result of the projects – including voluntary and community-based work which has helped contribute to the maintenance of the estate, or supported further local activities for residents.

employers, including problem solving, communication skills, and team-working. The role of the arts in building confidence, motivation and self-esteem also emerges as an important factor in creating routes through to further education and employment.

The types of skills fostered by arts activities are increasingly relevant in todays jobs market. The creative industries have been identified as one of the fastest growing sectors in the UKs economy, expanding at twice the rate of the economy as a whole, and already contributing 8% of gross value added nationally. The term creative industries is defined by government to include the visual arts and design, architecture, music, publishing, the performing arts, interactive leisure software, film and broadcast industries. At a time when traditional employment sectors like manufacturing are declining, more new jobs are being created in these fields than in others, with current employment at approximately 1.9 million people (Creative Industries Economic Estimates August 2004, DCMS). As the Prime Minister argued in his foreword to the Government Green Paper *Culture and Creativity: The Next Ten Years*, this means that creative talent will be crucial to our individual and national economic success in the economy of the future. (DCMS (b) 2001: 3)

Regional Development Agencies and local authorities have been quick to recognise the growing importance of the creative industries, and the wider role of the arts and culture in regeneration. Many have supported area-based studies of the sector – for example *Employing Creativity: Skills Development in the North West of England* published by the Northwest Development Agency in 2002, which highlights the role of creative learning in providing routes into employment, and *Creative London* published by the London Development Agency in 2004. In addition to undertaking relevant research, regional and local government agencies often provide direct support to local organisations which specialise in arts development and training, and these can be well-placed to work in community, school or housing settings.

The case studies described later in this guide have offered a variety of creative learning and participatory opportunities to residents. These range from music and video production (Isle of Wight) to internet and broadcast technologies (Liverpool and Birmingham) and design, photography and computer graphics (Look Ahead, Newbold and Plymouth). They have done this by enabling residents to work alongside professional artists in workshops and on practical projects, through partnerships with local colleges, and through the provision of equipment, venues and materials for use by local residents. Many participants have gone on to access further learning, education or employment as a direct result of the projects – including voluntary and community-based work which has helped contribute to the maintenance of the estate, or supported further local activities for residents.

Reducing crime and anti-social behaviour

There has been a number of evaluations of community-based cultural activities involving young people at risk of exclusion which have shown marked benefits in helping to reduce anti-social behaviour and criminal activity. Evaluations of the Summer Plus and Splash Extra schemes (now known as Positive Activities for Young People), which provided access to the arts and sport for young people at risk, showed that 71% of participants return to education and 6% to employment or training. The number of breaches of statutory orders decreased by 16% in the areas where the scheme ran, compared with a 12% increase elsewhere, and there was a general reduction in youth crime rates. In Avon and Somerset the Splash scheme saw a 31% reduction in robberies compared with a 56% increase in areas where the scheme didnt run. (Cap Gemini Ernst & Young 2003)

In a 2003 review by the Unit for Arts and Offenders into the value and role of the arts in criminal justice programmes, the authors examined fifteen case studies between 1989 and 2002, including the Splash Extra programme referred to above. Case studies included music, poetry and theatre workshops for community residents and young people in areas of high crime (Hull Cop Shop); and a film project with young people at high risk of offending on a deprived estate (The Openshaw Uncovered Project). Respectively, outcomes suggested:

- 60-80% reduction in burglary
- 65-78% reduction in youths causing annoyance
- the building of positive relationships between young people, adults and police
- a direct and indirect impact on the social and psychological aspects of young peoples experience of social exclusion
- young people were supported in developing a sense of self-worth

(The Unit for the Arts and Offenders, 2003)

Engaging young people creatively in designing and making physical improvements to public spaces is another approach which has been shown to lead to long-term reductions in the levels of graffiti and vandalism in an area. Well-designed public spaces can also help reduce the fear of crime and improve the quality of life for all residents. Case studies like the Northmoor Urban Art Project, *Tackling Fear of Crime Through Art*, described later in this guide, bear this out.

The research studies noted above are useful in providing a more objective body of evidence, to support the numerous anecdotal reports about the changes which arts projects can deliver at a local level. When taken together, they present a list of potential benefits:

- developed self confidence and self esteem
- increased creativity and motivation
- improved skills in planning and organising activities
- improved communication of ideas and information
- raised or enhanced educational attainment

Engaging young people creatively in designing and making physical improvements to public spaces is another approach which has been shown to lead to long-term reductions in the levels of graffiti and vandalism in an area.

19

- increased appreciation of the arts
- created social capital
- developed community identity, tolerance and cohesion
- decreased social isolation
- improved understanding of different cultures
- promoted interest in the local environment
- activated social change
- raised public awareness of an issue
- enhanced mental and physical health and well-being
- reduced offending and anti-social behaviour
- increased the employability of individuals

The growing body of evidence in this field suggests that housing associations should not view community arts projects as peripheral to their work, but consider support for the arts as a core part of any community development strategy or tenant participation project.

20

While not all projects will produce all of these outcomes, the length of this list reflects some of the inherent strengths of arts projects – their diversity and adaptability. Rather than following a formula, arts projects are unique in that they can be delivered via a wide variety of mediums, developed in consultation with local people, and can respond to a particular context or community.

The growing body of evidence in this field suggests that housing associations should not view community arts projects as peripheral to their work, but consider support for the arts as a core part of any community development strategy or resident participation project. The Housing Corporation's *Involvement Policy for the Housing Association Sector* (2004) advises housing associations to explore more innovative approaches to resident participation, and to provide more choice in ways to involve residents. A growing number of social housing organisations are already using arts and cultural activities as a means of achieving this. These organisations have well-developed arts strategies in place, employ dedicated staff, and support on-going programmes of activity.

In this guide it has only been possible to select a few from the many examples of successful arts projects led by housing or residents' associations in England and Wales. We have focused on individual projects, even when these form part of wider programmes of arts activity. Case studies have been chosen to illustrate the range and diversity of projects, their achievements, and how they have been delivered in different contexts and regions. They include participatory activities in music, film, crafts, painting, design, performance and broadcasting. Some have involved the provision of community buildings and facilities for cultural use. Many have involved partnerships with local colleges and arts organisations. Some have focused on delivering physical improvements to estates through public artworks, or artists engagement in the design process. Others have aimed to support community cohesion and consultation during major refurbishment programmes. All case studies were researched during 2003 and are based on interviews held with residents, staff and artists.

... many housing associations are beginning to look beyond formal mechanisms and exploring more imaginative ways of involving residents in local regeneration initiatives.

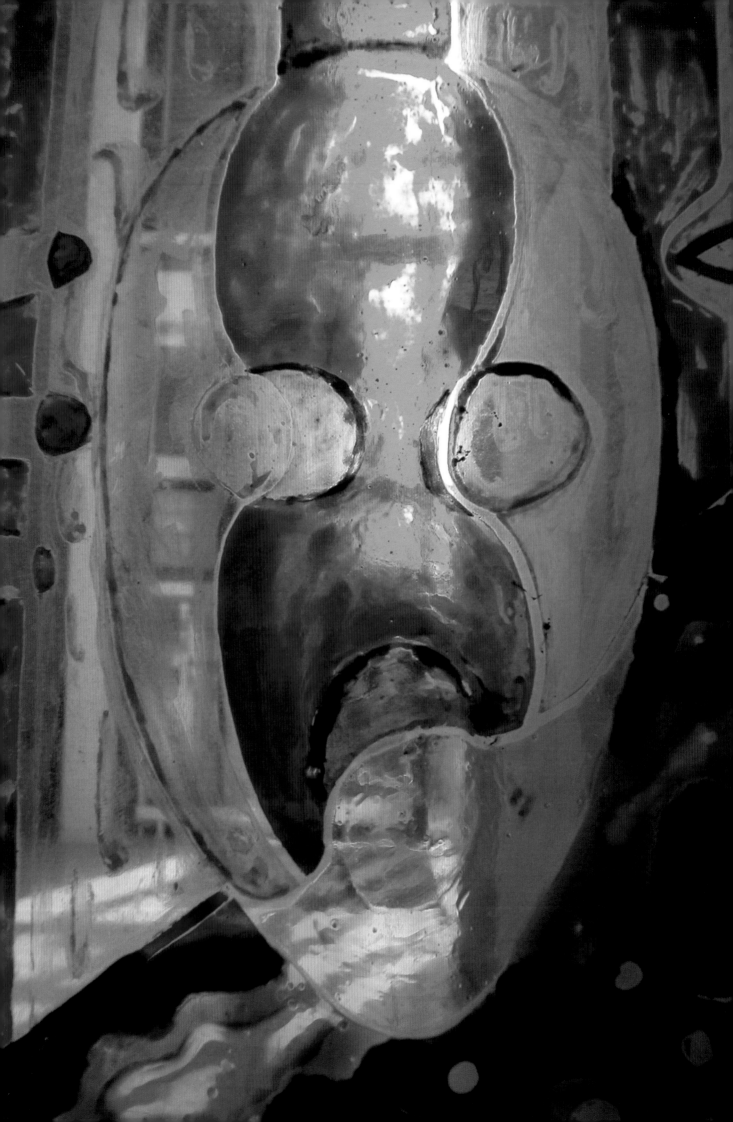

case studies

examples of art projects helping to
build sustainable communities

"As a result of the Neighbourhood Watching film project, people on the estate appear to communicate with each other more."

Michael Needham, Project leader

neighbourhood watching
st peter's estate, bethnal green, london

24

Introduction

The St Peter's Estate, built in 1967, is located in Bethnal Green in the London Borough of Tower Hamlets. It consists of five concrete framed, six-storey deck-access blocks containing 176 flats. Three blocks surround a main courtyard, the other two blocks share a communal grassed area.

Tower Hamlets is the smallest London borough, covering less than eight square miles. The population is ethnically diverse. According to the latest census figures almost half (48%) of the population are from black and minority ethnic groups. The largest of these groups is Bangladeshi residents, who make up 34% of the borough's population and are the single largest minority ethnic population in London (Borough Profile 2003, London Borough of Tower Hamlets). 43% of residents in Tower Hamlets are claiming Income Support. The St Peter's Ward (now Bethnal Green North) ranked at

313 in the national index of multiple deprivation in 2000 (DETR, 2000) of the 8,414 wards nationally.

The age and condition of the housing stock, along with a serious overcrowding problem, had long been a concern in the borough. In order to meet Decent Home Standards by 2010, the local council, through its Housing Choice programme, consulted residents on the potential transfer of a large number of its properties to registered social landlords. The St Peter's Estate residents voted to proceed to stage two of that process and set up a steering group to meet prospective landlords. However, there proved to be real difficulties engaging residents in the consultation process, and although there was a Tenants and Residents' Association on the estate, the committee was made up of only four residents prior to the start of the arts project.

An important element of the project
was to involve local artists working
with the community

The arts project

In September 2001, the St Peter's Square Tenants and Resident's Association was concerned about the lack of attendance at meetings, and was considering ways of raising its profile among residents. The courtyard at the heart of the estate had suffered many years of neglect, and had come to symbolise the overall decline of the neighbourhood. Committee member Michael Needham, combining his interest in film and the visual arts, proposed that the courtyard be used as a space for a community screening. His idea was to convert it into an inner-city amphitheatre, where residents could view short films, animations and archive footage from front doors and balconies. He suggested putting together a

programme of films that were uniquely related to the setting, the buildings, the interests of the community, and the cultural diversity of local residents.

The committee agreed the proposal, and permission for use of the courtyard was obtained from the borough council through the local estate office. At this stage the Tenants and Resident's Association was able to put together a project plan, and successfully applied for funding from London Arts (now Arts Council England, London) and Awards for All, as well as contributing from their own group's funds. They consulted residents widely, through a letter and poster campaign, which was followed up with a press release.

"This was the beginnings of a dialogue with the area, with the structures, with the culture, with the people, with the buildings."

The Rev. John Weir, Vicar of St Peter's

An important element of the project was to involve local artists working with the community, and so Ashley McCormick and Rayna Nadeem were commissioned in this capacity. They produced works ranging from video portraits of residents, to animations advertising local businesses which were drawn and narrated by children from the nearby Elizabeth Selby Infants School. Michael Needham made a short film featuring Bethnal Green residents and locations: *My Familiar Place*. One of the films, *A Love Supreme*, focused on a pair of hands as they made samosas. The hands belonged to the mother of the film's director Nilesh Patel. In describing its aims, he said:

> *"Samosas are familiar to everyone in London, and I hope Asian and non-Asian members of the audience will have appreciated the skill and artistry involved in their creation."*

An audience vote revealed *Lift* as people's favourite, a striking documentary made by Marc Isaacs in the lift of Denning Point, a local tower block. The chairs for the event were loaned by St Peter's church, and a local Indian restaurant provided bhajis and samosas.

The committee was astounded by the project's success, and by the local and national attention it received. *The Guardian* wrote a review in its *Society* section (September 18th), and *Vertigo*, the independent film magazine, included a profile in its autumn edition.

Michael Needham subsequently incorporated Neighbourhood Watching as a non-profit making organisation, and received a further commission for a screening on a Peabody Trust Estate in Westminster in September 2003. Neighbourhood Watching has since led a number of local projects within Tower Hamlets, notably a mobile bingo project for Tower Hamlets Housing Action Trust, a video-workshop with young people and a pyrotechnic workshop for over 16s, both funded by Oxford House in Bethnal Green.

As a result of the Neighbourhood Watching film project, people on the estate appear to communicate with each other more. There is more involvement in the activities of the Tenants and Resident's Association, and two new members have joined the committee. The local authority's support and involvement has meant that the relationship between residents and the borough council also appears to have improved. With so many council estates being transferred to new landlords and the danger of what Michael sees as the breaking up of housing estates into separate communities, he believes that Neighbourhood Watching helped promote community spirit and bring people together at a time of change and uncertainty.

"You can have very well-meaning projects that go disastrously wrong because people aren't consulted enough. But what we liked about this was how carefully the consultation was planned."

Peter Cross, Visual Arts Officer, Arts Council England

"The beauty of the event was that the space was the main focus. The local Bengali women who normally cannot participate in community events were able to stand on their balconies and find out about their neighbours."

Michael Needham

Summary

Name of project
Neighbourhood Watching.

Project leader
Michael Needham.

Cost of the project
£14,000.

Length of the project
Ten months, and three months to plan.

How was the project funded?
London Arts £9,000.
Awards For All £4,900.
Tenants and Resident's Association £100.
In-kind support from the local church, businesses and film production companies.

Whose idea was the project?
Michael Needham and the Tenants & Resident's Association.

How was it organised?
The Tenants and Resident's Association planned and organised everything, starting with thorough community consultation.

How were the community attracted to the project?
Through a press release, letters to every resident, and posters. Two artists were commissioned to work with residents to produce short films, video portraits, and animations. Vox pop style interviews with residents were held on the estate, which helped to engage the community.

Who participated in the project?
Local residents, the Tenants and Resident's Association Committee, the local infant school, the local authority, the artists, the local church and small businesses.

Was it a wider section of the community than would otherwise have been involved?
Yes, especially black and minority ethnic residents who do not normally become involved in other Tenants and Resident's Association activities.

What did the organisation expect to get out of the project?
To raise the profile of the Tenants and Resident's Association on the estate, to encourage more involvement in the committee by other residents, and more communication between residents on the estate.

What were the outcomes?
All of the above. It has helped bring people together at a time of change and uncertainty. Neighbourhood Watching is now a company in its own right, delivering similar projects for other landlords and continuing to work on the St Peter's Estate and

participate in other consultation exercises held by the borough council. There is now an improved relationship between local residents and the council and Neighbourhood Watching is also recognised for its work by the Local Area Partnership.

Were they the expected outcomes?
More than expected.

Did the community learn any new skills from the project?
The committee learnt project management, budgeting, fundraising, communication and negotiating skills. Children involved learned animation and drawing skills.

Was there a difference between the planned and final costs?
No.

Has it made a difference to community engagement in other aspects of regeneration?
It is still too early to tell. But it has improved communication and interaction in the community, and because of this the housing office also see the estate in a different light now.

On a scale of 1-10 how would you rate the success of the project for the organisation and the community (1 being poor, 10 being excellent)?
9.

Website: www.neighbourhoodwatching.co.uk

*"People still talk about the
photography project positively."*

Rachel Wolstenholme, Guinness Trust

images of newbold
newbold estate, rochdale

Introduction

The Newbold Estate is located in inner Rochdale and consists of 2000 low rise, mostly traditional terraces, in a ward which ranks among the 5% most deprived wards in England (DETR, 2000). Newbold has the second highest unemployment and child poverty rates in the country, and is perceived as one of the crime hot-spots in the Rochdale area. 445 of the properties on the estate are 1970s built, and owned and managed by the Guinness Trust.

In 1999 a survey of the estate revealed concerns about crime and disorder among residents, and a desire for more community activities which could offer choice for a range of different groups. Further research commissioned by the Guinness Trust in 2000 identified that 16.8% of the people in Newbold classed themselves as of Asian background. The research concluded that while the Asian population was growing, there was little interaction other residents in the area.

Newbold is located within a central Rochdale Single Regeneration Budget (SRB5) programme: Revitalising Inner Rochdale. This seven-year programme (1999-2006) funds projects delivering physical improvements, business support, lifelong learning, health and leisure opportunities, and community capacity-building. One strand of the funding goes towards the *Revitalising Inner Rochdale Cultural Programme*, which was created to support agencies in inner Rochdale to develop methods of using cultural and arts activities to enhance the delivery of their aims and objectives.

The Involving Communities Programme Team reported less participation by Newbold residents in open meetings than other wards in the regeneration programme. Subsequently, European Regional Development Fund (ERDF) Objective 2 funding was used to support a community development worker based in Newbold to assist in the creation of local community groups and increase the level of community participation in regeneration activities. This helped establish a local resident group, NewTrac, and the Guinness Trust donated a house for use as its community base.

The arts project

The SRB Cultural Programme invested in a pilot arts project between March and May 2002 involving the Guinness Trust, NewTrac (the local residents' group), SureStart, young travellers and members of the local youth group. Each group worked with a familiar community worker and professional photographer to take digital images of areas of their neighbourhood that were important to them – for both positive and negative reasons. The objectives of the pilot project were:

- to improve understanding and cohesion between culturally diverse residents on the Newbold Estate and particularly between the white residents and those of South-Asian origin or descent
- to increase local interest and involvement in community activities, regeneration and consultation projects
- establish the practice of arts-based consultation and participation
- increase interest in the arts as an educational or career choice.

Forty residents became directly involved in the project, although only twenty-six had attended a local community information day earlier in the year. Crucially, a real mixture of residents were involved, including 'hard to reach' groups, young people, travellers and South Asian women. The project

32

The pilot project produced such positive feedback and interest from participants that the Guinness Trust decided to become more involved in future arts projects as a way of enhancing their community development initiatives.

encouraged people to use the arts to expand into new areas of involvement.

During the project, residents researched and discussed ideas about their environment, and worked in small groups with a professional artist to produce and present images that communicated these ideas, featuring local places and people. Participants gained experience of using cameras and computer graphics and showed a genuine interest in the work. The final photographic boards were presented at an exhibition in the town hall, where residents had the opportunity to present their work and help promote Newbold in a positive way. The event brought together members

from different parts of the community, and was the first time many of them had interacted.

The pilot project produced such positive feedback and interest from participants that the Guinness Trust decided to become more involved in future arts projects as a way of enhancing their community development initiatives. With support from the SRB Cultural Programme they have developed ideas for a two-year arts project, Engaging Newbold, using visual arts and creative writing to deliver work with a range of people. The Trust has taken a lead in further fundraising and made a commitment to manage the project and artists.

*"People are now positive about art
– so we said 'Go for it!'"*

Rachel Wolstenholme, Guinness Trust

"The children have soaked it up like a sponge."

Jacqui Holmes, Community Development Worker

Summary

Name of project
Images of Newbold.

Organisation
Guinness Trust.

Project leader
Zoe Higgens, Cultural Project Co-Ordinator.

Total cost of project
£3,500.

Length of the project
2 months including 1 month in planning.

How was the project funded?
Single Regeneration Budget.
The Guinness Trust (paid for the Community
Development Worker's involvement).

Whose idea was the project?
It was a collective idea, which initially came out of
discussions between youth workers and young
people.

How was it organised?
By Zoe Higgens in partnership with a multi-agency
group. The project employed a local arts organisation
to commission an artist to work with each of the
four resident groups and a staff member.

How were the community attracted to the project?
Through workers based on the estate, door-knocking
and word of mouth. Community involvement was
planned by the various agencies involved in the
project, working in partnership.

Who participated in the project?
Guinness Trust, NewTrac residents' association, the
travellers' service, the local authority's Youth Service
and SureStart. The project attracted a mix of
residents including the young, elderly, different
ethnic groups and travellers.

How many people in total did it involve?
40 residents.

*Was it a wider section of the community than would
otherwise have been involved?*
Yes, definitely.

*What did the organisations expect to get out of the
project?*
They hoped to improve understanding between
culturally diverse residents on the estate, increase
involvement in regeneration initiatives, provide arts
activities of interest to tenants, and help tenants to
express themselves and learn new skills.

What were the outcomes?
All of the above. The project also encouraged
people to expand into new areas of involvement,
and led to a commitment to fund future arts
activities on the estate.

Were they what the organisation expected?
They exceeded expectations and generated a lot of interest among the community.

Did the community learn any new skills from this project?
Photography, picture composition, digital image manipulation and software.

Was there a difference between the planned costs and final costs?
No.

Following this project, has it been easier to engage the community in other aspects of regeneration?
Yes, definitely. This project has led to further projects and got a lot more people interested and engaged in the regeneration process. It has resulted in an increased pride in the estate. It has had a symbiotic effect on the organisations' communication and interaction with the community.

Is there another or follow on project planned?
Yes – there is a long-term plan to develop a two-year arts programme, but small projects will also follow.

How will this be funded?
£15,000 from Community Cohesion, £3,500 from Lloyds TSB, £7,000 from SRB5.

On a scale of 1-10, how would you rate the success of the project for the organisation and the community (1 being poor, 10 being excellent)?
9 – very positive for the organisation.

On a scale of 1-10, how would you rate the value for money aspect of the project ?
10 – excellent, a winner.

"A lot of people are now working as a result of this project – they feel empowered."

Eddie Hanley, participant & local resident

36

pembroke street arts programme
devonport, plymouth

Introduction

Pembroke Street Estate was hurriedly built in 1955 as part of a post-war rebuilding programme in Devonport, a mile west of Plymouth city centre, in the St Peter's ward. It consists of 160 flats arranged in thirteen blocks, and is situated within a pedestrianised complex which forms part of Mount Wise, one of the most disadvantaged areas of Devonport.

Defence cuts and a lack of investment in the early 1980s led to massive job cuts that reduced the local dockyard workforce from nearly 15,000 to 5,000. As a result, what was once a thriving, confident community became one of the poorest wards in England, racked by youth crime, joyriding, vandalism, poor housing and unemployment.

By the late 1980s, the residents of Pembroke Street Estate had become increasingly despondent about their living conditions. Vandalism and general neglect were the norm. Broken glass, boarded windows and graffiti made the street and its surroundings drab and ugly. The Pembroke Resident Participation Group was formed in January 1987 by a small group of residents who felt that the time had come to do something positive to improve living conditions on the estate. The success of their initiatives quickly led to the setting up of an Estate Management Board to run the Estate in 1994. Physical improvements to the area began in1992 following a successful application for £6million Estate Action funding to improve internal and external areas.

The arts project

In 1993, Dee Evans, Plymouth Theatre Royal's Community Education Officer who had been working in the area suggested that Plymouth City Council apply its newly adopted Percent for Art policy to the Pembroke Street renewal programme. The policy was that a proportion of the budget for all major building and refurbishment programmes go towards arts initiatives to benefit local people. Because a 'percent for art' had not been set aside earlier in the planning process, residents met to look for savings elsewhere. They decided that they did not need toughened glass in the top floor windows of the blocks and so £70,000 was found to put towards the Pembroke Street public arts programme.

An experienced community arts consultant, Lesley Greene, was funded by the Theatre Royal to prepare a feasibility study. Having spent a day on the estate talking to residents, she put together a proposal which was accepted by both residents and City Council as a blueprint for the project. The idea was to weave artwork into the very fabric of the estate, ensuring a distinctive and coherent overall design. This would be done by engaging artists to work closely with the core planning and design team from the beginning of the project, and to engage the community in the process.

"It gets people talking to each other. If you said to people you have to talk to your neighbour, it can be like having your picture taken – you would not be able to relax. But if you start talking as part of a project, it is much easier and more natural."

Dave Ball, participant and local resident

38

Two artists, Tony and Glenn Eastman, were commissioned to lead the community consultation process in partnership with Plymouth College of Art and Design (now Plymouth University). Residents from each block found themselves engaged in discussion with architects, landscape architects, arts officers, design students and professional artists about every aspect of the refurbishment programme, including colours, signage, fencing, paths and even the naming of individual blocks. The history of Devonport was chosen as a theme to underpin the programme, which prompted a valuable exercise in researching and documenting the history of the area.

The project created unique metalwork designs for fencing and railings in each of the thirteen blocks and around the perimeter of the estate, distinctive metalwork gates to the carparks, school and utility areas, carved stone cappings on some of the brick pillars, and unusual block signs, mosaics and other artwork around the estate. The residents played a leading role in designing the artwork and in contributing to other elements of the refurbishment programme. Local artists, students and residents

gained employment and skills from the process – something which wouldn't have happened if less personalised fencing and signage had been purchased from a distant supplier. The public art programme added a vital element of local colour and distinctiveness to the refurbished estate.

Previously there had been very little arts activity in Devonport. The public art consultation and design process drew in many residents who had no prior interest in or experience of the visual arts or crafts. The project increased their understanding of and interest in the arts and in local history, as well as providing residents with new skills, which in some cases provided the groundwork for finding employment. The Estate Management Board believes residents communicate more as a result of the arts project and they now find it easier to get residents to meetings.

The initial project acted as a catalyst for further art activities, which have been incorporated into the Greenlink Community Environmental Arts Programme.

"Five years ago Pembroke Street people wouldn't have thought about the arts at all. They were just concerned about the threat of being burgled. Now when you wake up in the morning there is something really appealing to look at."

Christine Watts MBE, Co-ordinator, Pembroke Street Estate Management Board

Summary

Name of project
Pembroke Street Arts Programme.

Organisation
Pembroke Street Estate Management Board (EMB), Devonport, Plymouth.

Project leader
Dick Watson, Community Projects Consultant.

Total cost of project
£83,900.

Length of project
6 years, 1994-2000.

How was the project funded?
Estate Action & SRB funding, following the adoption of a 'percent for art' policy. Plymouth Theatre Royal supported the feasibility study and there was in-kind support from Plymouth College of Art and Design and Marks and Spencer.

Whose idea was the project?
The Estate Management Board, tenants and residents.

How long did it take to plan?
6 months.

How was it organised?
Pembroke Street Estate Management Board commissioned and monitored the project via a sub committee. They negotiated with Plymouth College of Art & Design to play a role in organising the project, with mutual benefits for students and residents. Professional artists were engaged to lead the consultation process.

How was the community attracted to the project?
Workshops, meetings and 'taster' sessions were arranged, and the project was embedded in the overall decanting and refurbishment programme for the estate. It was an open invitation to everyone to get involved. The use of a community flat was important, as it gave the project a base in the community.

Who participated in the project?
Tenants, residents, young people, secondments from Marks & Spencer, students from Plymouth College of Art & Design. Tony & Glenn Eastman were the artists whose special skill was engaging the community. Tony Dunne was the mosaic artist.

How many people in total did it involve?
100.

Was it a wider section of the community than would have otherwise been involved?
Yes, definitely. One third of the residents were over 60 but it also included young children (aged five and up), adults, and the unemployed (although more of these are now working as a result). It also included people from neighbouring estates.

What did the organisation expect to get out of the project?
The core aim was to brighten up the estate, create a sense of ownership and involve as many residents as possible in the project. It was also hoped that it would prevent vandalism on the estate by creating something of which the community would be proud.

What were the outputs/outcomes?
It has made a huge difference to the community. The estate is now brighter, more cheerful, and there is less vandalism. The Estate Management Board are now spending a lot less on vandalism, virtually next to nothing. There is also a renewed community spirit, people talk to each other more. Residents started off very cynically but as the projects were woven into the fabric of the refurbishment it changed their minds. Many people have got jobs through their involvement in the project – it engendered new confidence in themselves and their community. It also brought in people from other projects and resulted in a shared experience that would not normally have happened. It created a new commitment to improving the area.

40

St Stephen's House 77-99
100-122 Doyle House
Himalaya House 101-123
124-146 Alhambra House
Metropole House 125-147
148-170 Ashley House
Chinatown House 149-171
172-194 Royal Oak House
Monument House 173-195
196-218 Bacchus House
Sovereign House 197-219
220-242 Canterbury House
Albion House 16-46

"Expectations were exceeded."

Were they the expected outcomes/outputs?
Expectations were exceeded.

Did the community learn any new skills from this project?
Yes, this project provided opportunities to work with professional artists and learn new skills such as working with metal, mosaic, design, art, project planning and organisation. It gave people confidence and made them look at themselves in a different way and gave access to new areas of experience.

Was there a difference in the planned costs and final costs?
Difficult to say, things evolved, and some parts were more expensive and took longer. There were no real surprises.

Has it made a difference to community engagement in other aspects of regeneration?
People are more cheerful and much more confident with a renewed willingness to get involved with the Estate Management Board and its projects. They recently carried out a consultation on an unused

piece of adjacent land and out of 160 properties, 88 (55%) were represented at the meeting. There is now more connection with the community – it is easier to involve them in almost anything.

Is there another or follow on project planned?
The project directly led to a £900,000 lottery, ERDF and SRB funded Greenlink Community Environmental Arts Project, and provided the confidence and community networks to enable a bid for £50 million for New Deal for Communities Funding. The latter will fund a further significant urban regeneration and new housing programme. It has also led to a Cultural Plan for Devonport which is likely to support further projects of this kind.

On a scale of 1-10 how would you rate the success of the project for the organisation and the community (1 being poor, 10 being excellent)?
9 – it has lasted and improved.

On a scale of 1-10 how would you rate the value for money aspect of the project?
9 – excellent value for money.

41

"Consultation is far more effective if you use mediums such as art."

Robbie Davison, New Business Initiatives Manager

closer project
speke and garston, south liverpool

Introduction

South Liverpool Housing (SLH) manage 4,500 properties as a result of a housing stock transfer in 1999. Speke and Garston is home to some 25,000 people and about 10,000 of them live in a South Liverpool Housing home. Much of the housing in the area was first built to 'garden suburb' principles: solid homes with their own front and back gardens, a central shopping area and plenty of open space.

Unfortunately Speke and Garston became an area of significant deprivation and disadvantage. In 2002 Speke was identified as the second most deprived ward in the country and Garston (St Mary's ward) is ranked 86th in the index of multiple deprivation (DETR, 2000). Statistics indicate a high incidence of poverty and unemployment, low skills and low educational attainment.

Since the mid-1990s the Speke Garston Development Company and the Speke Garston Partnership, working with the private and public sectors, have attracted major investment to the area. The physical environment of the industrial and commercial zones has been transformed from its former derelict state,

the local economy is accelerating and job opportunities are increasing. Housing conditions are also improving, with South Liverpool Housing having undertaken a massive improvement programme. The area benefits from local Education Action Zone and SureStart initiatives and European funding. These have helped support new schools, training, shopping and leisure facilities.

However, the social, economic and educational environment that local people were living in still gave cause for major concern. Many local people, who had suffered years of disadvantage and seen millions spent on the regeneration of their area, believed the money had done more to line the pockets of professional consultants and bureaucrats than it had done for local people and employment. Many viewed the landscape improvements to Speke Boulevard, 'the southern gateway to the city', as an attempt to hide them and their lives away from commuters, the city and the new commercial developments nearby. This cynicism meant that resident participation in regeneration initiatives in the area had been particularly low prior to the Closer project.

"This project was excellent value for money – better and cheaper than marketing campaigns."

Robbie Davison, New Business Initiatives Manager

The arts project

The Closer project was an initiative led by South Liverpool Housing (SLH) in Speke and Garston, in partnership with locally based organisation Arts in Regeneration (AiR). The aims of the project were to create a framework for participation that would:

- increase levels of resident participation
- provide training and support for residents that would enable them to take part with confidence
- integrate into other regeneration initiatives, thereby continuing to develop skills and participant numbers beyond the life of the project

The arts programme was ambitious in scale. It consisted of six projects, each involving a professional artist working collaboratively with local people, and involved almost 600 residents over a six-month period. The projects were:

- a documentary video about the redevelopment of Burnage Close, produced with the involvement of residents. The documentary focused upon the story of the re-development from their perspective, and was scripted and acted by the residents
- a play area for under-fours designed in

partnership with an artist, SureStart and local residents
- an internet radio project, covering two sheltered housing units, which helped introduce new technology and teach new skills to some of the most isolated groups in the community
- the Tate House feasibility project, exploring the possibility of the conversion of two houses into a space for local and national artists to display work
- a history project, in which residents of Monkfield Way worked with a commissioned artist to investigate local history, especially in relation to the monks who used to live in the area
- a dance and drama project in which artists worked with children and adults to create performances using the theme of community pride and celebation. This culminated in a Closer celebration evening which also showcased the other projects

John Moores University undertook an evaluation of Closer and concluded that it had increased participation, changed residents' perceptions of South Liverpool Housing and increased community cohesion.

43

Summary

Name of project
Closer.

Organisation
South Liverpool Housing.

Project leader
Robbie Davison – New Business Initiatives Manager.

Total cost of the project
£158,000.

Length of the project
6 Months, May-Oct 2001.

Who funded the project?
£30,000 Housing Corporation – Community Training & Enabling Grant.
£30,000 Regional Arts Lottery Programme (Arts Council England).
£33,000 SureStart.
£10,000 Speke Garston Partnership SRB.
£10,000 Capital of Culture (Liverpool City Council).
£30,000 South Liverpool Housing.
£2,000 Cream (the nightclub).

Whose idea was the project?
Robbie Davison-New Business Initiatives Manager.
Clare McColgan – Arts in Regeneration Manager.
Julie Marsh – Community Development Worker.

How was it organised?
Through South Liverpool's Community Development Team. Robbie Davison and Julie Marsh planned and ran the project alongside Amanda Bracebridge from Arts in Regeneration.

How was the community engaged in the project?
Through face to face consultation, door-knocking and public meetings. Firstly South Liverpool Housing called public meetings but no one came, so they began a series of door knocking sessions around the area to tell people what it was all about. This was followed up with face to face interviews and small local meetings to get people involved.

Who participated in the project?
Tenants, residents, young people, the elderly, the community development team, Arts in Regeneration, artists. A complete spread of the community.

How many people in total did it involve?
560, and there was a steering group of 15 people.

Was it a wider section of the community than would otherwise have been involved?
Absolutely – there was a complete mixture of residents.

What did the lead organisation expect to get out of the project?
The core aim was to spread fun and enjoyment as well as creating more participative structures, promoting South Liverpool Housing as a community organisation and gaining a national profile for the community development work it was undertaking.

What were the outcomes/outputs?
Closer certainly raised the profile of South Liverpool Housing. There were six projects in total, and a big party was held to celebrate afterwards. People still talk about the party. Community focus groups were set up as a result of this project.

Were the outcomes as expected?
More than expected – people's reaction was amazing. Closer really pushed people's boundaries. For example, matching the 'silver surfers' with video equipment.

"It brought the community together so it was no longer a struggle to get people involved – now people trust us."

Robbie Davison, New Business Initiatives Manager

"People are very wary of authority whereas, this being art, it's been less formal and friendly, but it still got us where we wanted to go."

Resident

Did the community learn any new skills from this project?
Yes – information technology, internet, radio and video skills, drama, modelling, communication, social interaction, budgeting, meeting and organising skills.

Was there a difference in the planned costs and final costs?
South Liverpool Housing initially agreed to put in £20,000 but in the end the whole project went £25,000 over budget.

Has this project made a difference to community engagement in other aspects of regeneration?
Absolutely, this project brought the community together and achieved more in six months than previous regeneration initiatives had done in the past five years. Closer went out to see the people face to face and this made the difference. It has opened the door to new projects – South Liverpool Housing now believes art can be part of everything. This project increased participation, built up trust, brought in additional resources. It is now imbedded into the organisation's strategic direction and culture.

Is there another or follow on project planned?
Yes, South Liverpool Housing has lots of projects planned as part of its environmental strategy, and also wants to bring art into their development process. They are working with the Tate to create a purpose built arts facility. Residents are participating in the Your TV project – a new media project to give access to free-to-view digital channels and a community channel through a set top box.

How will this be funded?
Speke and Garston are part of a European Objective 1 area, so the funding will come from this as well as the Housing Corporation.

On a scale of 1-10, how would you rate the success of the project for the organisation and the community (1 being poor, 10 being excellent)?
10 – it has put South Liverpool Housing on the map.

On a scale of 1-10, how would you rate the value for money aspect of the project ?
10 – it is better and cheaper than marketing campaigns.

45

"We learnt new skills in writing and photography."

Ahmed Mohammed, participant

46

tenants in focus
taff housing association, cardiff

Introduction

Taff Housing Association is a community-based housing provider founded in 1975. Its mission is to provide quality homes and community services for people on low incomes in Cardiff. Taff Housing Association is an Industrial and Provident Society, with charitable rules. It is registered with the National Assembly of Wales as a registered social landlord. The association has flats, houses, and sheltered housing for older people in the Riverside, Canton, Grangetown and Fairwater areas of Cardiff. It currently manages approximately 900 units of accommodation, provides support for its own tenants and manages contracts with other housing providers in and around Cardiff. The association is a member of a group of housing associations called Grwp Agored. This group aims to bring associations together to help them share costs and improve the quality of their services, while maintaining the local focus for the work of each of the group's members.

In 2002, Taff Housing Association were looking for new ways for tenants to participate in decision making and develop their own skills. Tenant involvement was usually through meetings, events such as openings, and questionnaires.

Viv Jones

I was born in the last house, 29, on Robert Street, Ely. A width of the road away was a haystack and farm and the river 50 yards away, a most magnificent place to have been brought up in. The woods were a quarter of an hour's walk away. There was the farm to learn about animals on. There was haymaking, the river for swimming and diving, making your own canoes and boats. It was an adventurous playground.

There was the paper mill on the other side of the river, where there were large rolls of paper. We would take them and make paddles out of the paper, and float them out to Penarth. It was a wonderful place to grow up. I never had any childhood illnesses bar one. I can even remember the headmistress's desk in my school exactly as it was; the multicoloured pens,

The arts project

The Chief Executive, Elaine Ballard, conceived the idea of a combined photography and audio project that would:

- use photography as a medium for increasing tenant participation
- use audio recording and editing to enable tenants to express themselves, by gathering life stories and sharing them with others
- improve the self-esteem of tenants by enabling them to learn new skills, and celebrate their lives
- help make a photographic and narrative

record which could be used to promote a more positive image of social housing tenants.

Taff Housing Association discussed the project with its Tenant's Association and there was strong support from the Chair and members. With support from the Arts Council of Wales, two local artists, Mo Wilson and Brian Morgan, were commissioned to work with 20 residents and produce photographic and personal narrative works.

The project began with a launch event for participants, at which roles were explained, and a

"This project has benefited by linking us into the wider community, and word has spread of the Somali community."

Ahmed Mohammed, participant

48

visit to Llanover Hall Arts Centre to encourage interest in future arts training opportunities. The residents, who came from a wide range of cultural backgrounds, were invited to pair up and portray themselves in both images and words. They were shown how to use professional cameras and tape recording equipment and introduced to some of the skills used by photographers and story gatherers. The residents were asked to record personal stories that they felt best reflected their daily lives, with members of one household interviewing and photographing another. Several of Taff Housing Association's older Somali residents told moving stories about why they decided to stay in the Welsh capital.

The completed works were displayed collectively at an exhibition held from 8th April to 11th May 2003 in the Butetown History and Arts Centre, Cardiff Bay,

with the aim of giving the public an insight into the varied lives of those living in housing association homes across Cardiff. The works were also shown at a variety of other events, including the association's Annual General Meeting, a national housing conference, Taff's office and in Grwp Agored's annual report.

Project evaluation indicated that it increased participants' self esteem, generated interest in the arts, built confidence and led to an interest in taking computer and photo-editing courses. Through the casual interactions, participants made friends, and this led to an increase in the social capital of the area. One of the most notable outcomes of the project was that the Somali residents agreed to set up their own tenant's association to build further their relationship with their landlord and the wider community.

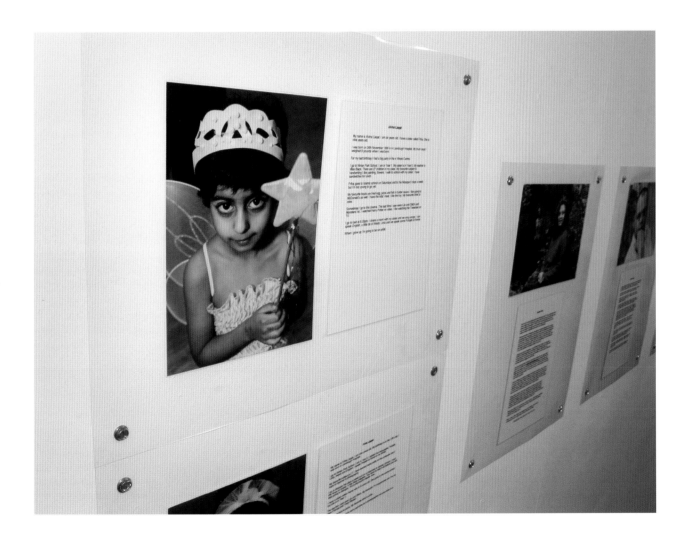

49

"A key objective in arranging this exhibition was to help
our residents become involved in arts activities while trying
to counter some of the public's negative perceptions of
housing associations and their tenants."

Elaine Ballard, Chief Executive, Taff Housing

"We made friends from our involvement in the project – it has put the Red Sea Café on the map."

Ahmed Mohammed, participant

Summary

Name of project
Tenants in Focus.

Organisation
TAFF Housing Association.

Project leader
Elaine Ballard, Chief Executive, TAFF Housing Association.

Total cost of project
£5,500.

Length of project
6 months and four weeks to plan.

How was the project funded?
£5,000 from the Arts Council of Wales.
£500 from TAFF Housing Association.

Whose idea was the project?
Elaine Ballard, Chief Executive TAFF Housing Association.

How was it organised?
Elaine Ballard planned and ran the project in collaboration with two local artists, Mo Wilson and Brian Morgan.

How was the community attracted to the project?
A description of the project was sent out to all residents, and volunteers were requested. It was also advertised in residents' newsletter and publicised by staff through everday contact with tenants, and using existing networks such as BME and community organisations to disseminate information. It was something different – a new approach because traditional participation approaches had produced limited results. This was a project that would help people acquire new skills and enable them to express themselves. It was an open invitation to everyone to get involved.

Who participated in the project?
14 tenants and residents from TAFF Housing Association and Cardiff City Council.

Was it a wider section of the community than would have otherwise would have been involved?
Yes definitely. This approach was especially helpful with attracting Somali elders to the project, who had previously been a difficult group to engage. One of the best outcomes is that there is now a Tenant's Association for the Somali community.

What did the organisation expect to get out of the project?
The core aims were to increase participation by trying something new and innovative for tenants and residents in which they are able to express themselves and learn new skills.

50

What were the outcomes?
Residents produced photographic portraits and a personal narrative about their lives. This led to the exhibition in the local arts centre, which helped change perceptions amongst the wider community. It improved participants' confidence, skills, and relationships within the community and with the housing association. It also led to the establishment of a Somali Tenant's Association.

Were the outcomes expected?
For the organisation they were much more than ever anticipated, and the setting up of a new Tenant's Association was a bonus.

Did the community learn any new skills from this project?
Yes – photography, story-telling, writing, communication and social skills.

Was there a difference between the planned and final costs?
Yes, extra costs were incurred for the launch at the arts centre, which took the project £150 over the original budget.

Has this project made a difference to the community?
Yes, definitely. They all enjoyed the project and have made new friends. As a result the Somali Community's Red Sea Café has seen an increase in customers and is now attracting non-Somali customers, which is a dream come true for the community. It has led to people being more sociable and has resulted in a lot of pride being generated in the community through the belief that they have achieved something. People are now interacting a lot more on a social level.

Is there another or follow on project planned?
Yes.

How will this be funded?
Arts Council of Wales or TAFF's Community Initiatives budget.

"We thought it would be great to involve tenants with each other working together to tell their own story."

Brian Morgan, artist involved in the project

On a scale of 1-10, how would you rate the success of the project for the organisation and the community (1 being poor, 10 being excellent)?
8.

On a scale of 1-10 how would you rate the value for money aspect of the project?
9.

"Everyone was involved."

June Booth, Residents' Association

all saints play area
farnworth, bolton

Introduction

Bolton has a population of 268,000 and is located 13 miles north-west of Manchester. The decline of the area's textile and engineering industries, which had long been the major sources of employment and wealth, created widespread levels of deprivation. Currently 48% of Bolton's population live in the worst twenty-five percent of deprived wards in the country (DETR, 2000).

Bolton Metropolitan Borough Council (Bolton MBC) and their partners have been keen to promote work, training, education and employment opportunities that are more relevant to today's economy, and have recognised the increasing expansion of the creative industries, which employ more people than mining, steel and car manufacture combined.

In terms of housing, the council began to recognise that the crime and anti-social behaviour in the area was partly attributable to the utilitarian, 'value for money' building culture of the early 1990s. To tackle this, they believed that a commitment to regenerating housing stock in partnership with existing tenants was key. This would require better consultation and dialogue with tenants. Efforts to realise this led to a growing appreciation of the role of the arts within housing regeneration schemes across separate sections of the council.

The 1990s saw a growth in the employment of artists on various projects. In the early stages they were brought in to discuss street furniture, architectural detail and placing of features such as mosaics and wrought iron work. Key officers and members were impressed by the way in which they contributed to community development, capacity building, and the popularity of schemes. In 1997 the Housing Committee at Bolton MBC agreed that 1% of its capital budget should be committed annually to arts initiatives within regeneration programmes. In 1999 the scheme was expanded with financial support from the ERDF. Bolton's flagship enabling partnership, Bolton Community Homes, (a partnership of Bolton MBC and nine local housing associations) agreed to participate in the initiative and make available 1% of the partners' capital budgets to community arts projects in Bolton – creating a combined annual budget, including staff costs, of approximately £400,000.

The Housing Percent For Art service is located directly within the Regeneration Unit of Bolton at Home, an Arms Length Management Organisation (ALMO). It consists of one full-time and two part-time members of staff housed in the Oxford Grove Urban Care (UCAN) Centre. Such has been the success of the scheme that in January 2004 a strategy was

"A brick company, Ibstock Bricks, put in the equivalent – through sponsorship-in-kind of £10,000 ... The Leisure Department was especially far sighted and they helped with the playground equipment and the surface."

June Booth, Residents Association

53

approved to increase the remit and resources of the team and create a further 3 full-time posts.

The service provides financial support and facilitates the management of the following participatory projects:

- arts-led consultation
- physical public art works
- celebratory and performance work
- business development for local artists
- community development through the arts
- artist input into new developments.

One of the Percent For Art scheme's earliest projects was the All Saints Playground. The All Saints Estate is in Farnworth, within the Bolton Metropolitan District. It was initially managed by the council but in November 2002 transferred to Bolton at Home. The estate is made up of 68 two-and three-bedroom 1960s terraced houses located adjacent to a small play area. The All Saints Resident's Group had no sense of ownership of the play area, there had been no consultation when it was first installed, and it had deteriorated rapidly.

"I was down at All Saints School the other day collecting one of the grandchildren when a little boy came up to me and said 'Mrs. Booth, it's you who owns our playground isn't it?' He was seven and looked very innocent. 'No,' I said, 'it's you who owns the playground."

June Booth Residents' Association

54

The arts project

In 1998 the resident's association heard that there was some 'art' money available and a steering group was formed including residents, housing and parks officers to develop a proposal. A £12,250 grant from the Percent for Art fund was approved and Jan Harley, an artist from Yorkshire was chosen (later joined by local shadowing artist Tracy McKay). In January 1999 she started work.

The brief for the artist was to consult and involve residents in the refurbishment of the play area to the specification of local residents; in design and creation of artworks; and in input into designs of railings and seating. A steering group was established and residents were recruited and consulted through surveys and door knocking. A venue for children's workshops was set-up in a local school and a workshop for adults was set up in the local scout hut. Group sessions started with discussion but soon

moved to hands-on work, including brick design, carving and firing. A brick company, Ibstock Bricks, put in the equivalent – through sponsorship in kind – of £10,000.

The project resulted in a well-used, well-managed and well-maintained play area, including a relief ceramic sculpture and brickwork designed and made by local children. The project exceeded the expectations of both the council and participants. Local residents started taking ownership of the play area, keeping it tidy and clean and securing it against vandalism. It facilitated a sense of community cohesion, built confidence and empowered residents. The project also improved communication between residents, the local housing officer, the council, local youths and other groups. The resident's association is now one of the main advocates of the Percent for Art process.

"Looking back, the thing I like the most about the complex process was that we were in complete control of the entire operation."

Dave Booth, Residents' Association

Summary

Name of project
All Saints Play Area.

Organisation
Bolton at Home, Bolton Metropolitan District Council, All Saints Residents' Association.

Project leader
Dave Booth.

Total cost of project
£59,000.

Length of project
12 Months (from 1999) and 3 months planning.

How was the project funded?
£17,000 Bolton Housing's Percent for Art scheme.
£19,000 Bolton MBC's Leisure Department.
£12,000 capital contribution from Bolton MBC's Housing Department.
£900 Bolton MBC's Creative Industries Development Team (Economic Regeneration).
£10,000 in kind, Ibstock Bricks Ltd.

Whose idea was the project?
The Residents' Association in discussion with the Percent for Art officer.

How was it organised?
A steering group met every two weeks, involving the Housing Officer, Parks Officer, the Housing Arts Officer and local residents. The artist organised the workshops and community engagement.

How did you attract the community to it?
Through Residents' Association meetings, artist-led workshops, the steering group, word of mouth and door knocking.

Who participated in the project?
Local residents, the school, church, youth club, council officers and members of the traveller community.

How many people in total did it involve?
200.

Was it a wider section of the community than would have otherwise would have been involved?
Yes, definitely, this project involved a very wide range of people including residents of a local travellers' site.

What were the outcomes?
The project led to the complete refurbishment of the play area with design input by local residents, including a relief ceramic sculpture, carved brickwork, railings and seating. There was an opening event with a song written by children at the local school. The project greatly improved communication between residents and the Housing Officer. Local residents started taking ownership of the play area, keeping it tidy and clean and preventing damage. It also improved relationships between youths and other groups. The Resident's Association is now an advocate for the Percent for Art scheme.

Were the outcomes as expected?
Exceeded expectations.

Did the community learn any new skills from this project?
Yes, representing their case to the council, negotiating skills, dealing with youth and learning that they can make things happen.

Was there a difference in the planned costs and final costs?
Yes, the budget increased to take account of new fencing for the play area.

Has this project made a difference to the community?
Yes definitely. It helped the community to gel, helped with social inclusion and the community now have a well-used, well-managed and well-maintained play area. Local residents now interact much better, the play area has become a focus for the community and is looked after by the local community.

"... we got down to making a lino-cut before starting to think how that design could be carved as a pattern on brick."

Tracy McKay, artist

57

Has it helped engage the community in other aspects of regeneration?
Yes it has – there is now a representative local group to consult with. It also had the effect of involving residents in cleaning up an adjacent tunnel area. Residents now put up hanging baskets and get involved in running a local festival funday.

Is there another or follow on project planned?
The Housing Officer has commented that he now gets calls saying, 'I've got an idea to improve area' rather than endless complaints. No immediate follow up is planned but there will be ongoing support for

environmental activities. For example, the All Saints Resident's Association recently produced a banner for the Bolton Mela, which is an Asian festival.

On a scale of 1-10, how would you rate the success of the project for the organisation and the community (1 being poor, 10 being excellent)?
9.

On a scale of 1-10, how would you rate the value for money aspect of the project ?
9 – it brought about greater social cohesion.

> *"You have made an impression that directly hits the point."*
>
> **Participant**

I love my little flat
attwood green estate, birmingham

Introduction

The Attwood Green Estate is adjacent to the central retail area of Birmingham City Centre and contains 2,800 properties. In the late 1990s it was dogged by deteriorating housing stock, a negative external image, social isolation among residents, a lack of community facilities and by a declining population. In 1998 residents voted with a clear majority (62.1%) to transfer stock to from direct management by Birmingham City Council to an independent and charitable social landlord, Optima Community Housing Association.

Optima were funded through the government's Estates Renewal Challenge Fund (ERCF) to undertake a £50 million building and refurbishment programme on the estate. This involved the demolition of 900 properties, their replacement with over 750 new homes, and the refurbishment of the 1,900 remaining properties across the five estates of Attwood Green. Optima were committed to ensuring residents were as fully informed and engaged in the planning and consultation process as possible, and were keen to find ways of supporting communications during a period of major change. They already provided resources to each of the residents' associations on the estate. Despite this there were difficulties engaging some people in the consultation processes and many felt alienated from the more formal decision-making structures. The disruption caused by major physical changes and the need to temporarily move people out of their homes can create anxiety and uncertainty – even hostility – to those perceived as responsible for the changes. A new mechanism was needed for people to express their opinions anonymously.

The artist went door-knocking to meet residents and tell them about the project.

The residency culminated in an exhibition at a flat ... called I Love My Little Flat.

59

The arts project

Optima was identified by the regional office of Arts Council England (then called West Midlands Arts) as a suitable agency to host and manage an artist-in-residence project as part of the 'Enabling Inclusion' gateway of their New Audiences Programme. The intention of the project was to employ an artist who was not immediately associated with Optima, who could live within the community and who could open new, more creative channels of communication with residents.

The artist's brief was drawn up by the Community Arts Co-ordinator for Optima with advice from Arts Council England. The brief was developed to be non-prescriptive with regard to artform, media or process. The post was advertised on the Arts Council's bulletin board and website and through various networks and mailing lists, including those of Birmingham City Council's Community Arts Department. A first stage interview panel was made up of a representative from Arts Council England, Optima's Community Arts Co-ordinator and the Arts Regeneration Officer of Birmingham City Council. The six proposals shortlisted included artists working in text, carnival arts, a film-maker and an artists' collective. Two were invited back to give presentations to a wider group of stakeholders including the tenant's association, the developer and Optima's resident liaison officers. They appointed Louise Teal, an artist experienced in group and community-based projects, who worked across film, video and photography.

The project took place between March 2002 and April 2003 and was managed by Optima's

Community Arts Co-ordinator. The artist designed the residency to maximise resident involvement through research, consultation, discussion, workshops and the production of artworks and events. Optima Community Housing Association helped with publicity by producing and distributing postcards across the estate with the artist's name, telephone number and e-mail address. The artist went door-knocking to meet residents and tell them about the project.

The artist worked primarily as 'facilitator' for the participants, using art as a vehicle for discussion, communication and to express the opinions of residents. Works produced included photo-collages and a tablecloth with images and texts illustrating their feelings about the regeneration process. The residency culminated in an exhibition at a flat, which was transformed to create a venue for a multi-media installation called *I Love My Little Flat*.

Summary

Name of project
I Love My Little Flat.

Organisation
Optima Community Housing Association.

Project leader
Optima Community Arts Co-ordinator.

Total cost of project
£30,000.

Length of project
The arts programme on the estate began in November 2001 following a successful application to the Arts Council's Regional Arts Lottery Programme (RALP) fund to help support a full-time post of Arts Co-ordinator within Optima. The project *I Love my Little Flat* by artist Louise Teal started in March 2002 and finished in April 2003.

How was is funded?
Arts Council England £20,000.
Optima £10,000.

How was it organised?
The project was planned by the artist, Louise Teal, and the Arts Coordinator for Optima Housing Association, and run by the resident's association with the support of the Arts Coordinator.

How was the community attracted to it?
Through the resident's association and a residents' arts advisory group who were committed to supporting the wider arts programme within the community. The community were engaged through the selection and planning process, word-of-mouth, postcards and printed materials, door-knocking, workshops, events and the artist's presence in the community.

Who participated in the project?
Approximately 120 adult residents participated (including 10 members of the Woodview Women's Group who worked with the artist over five weeks), 25 pupils from year eight of the local school, and eight young people from local youth club who took part in a video workshop. 200 residents attended the final exhibition.

Was it a wider section of the community than would otherwise have been involved?
Yes, it attracted people who did not engage in the resident's association or formal committees and consultations, including hard-to-reach groups like single parents and young people.

What did the organisation expect to get out of the project?
The project aimed to establish new networks and consultation structures which would engage the

"The artists intermediary role was very helpful. She offered residents a way to talk to Optima outside the normal channels. Optima had the opportunity to listen again; to hear people beyond the limited frameworks offered by our consultation network."

Community Arts Co-ordinator

community in the refurbishment and building programme and have a positive impact on the regeneration of the area and the cultural and social environment.

What were the outcomes?
The project produced a series of temporary and permanent art installations, projects and events which helped develop sustainable links within the community, provide new learning opportunities and cultural experiences for residents, open channels of communication with the housing association, and contribute to the living environment on the estate. It also helped strengthen cross-departmental communication within the housing association and support for creative approaches to resident participation and consultation.

Were they as expected?
The unexpected outcomes are often the small incidental events, connections or responses that you cannot plan for. For example, a person who has been depressed or feeling lonely or isolated can suddenly feel inspired. You can plan a session with local people but suddenly emotions can start to run high and you get more than you expected from the group, but it is cathartic for the participants. Responses to artworks can be difficult to plan for. The positive outcome for controversial art is it gets people thinking and talking about their area.

Did the community learn any new skills from this project?
It was more about new experiences.

Has this project made a difference to the community and their engagement in other aspects of regeneration?
Yes – people still talk about it with fondness. It has become a part of the collective memory for local people who took part. It has enabled other projects to happen and developed an openness in the community to try new things and to be brave about accepting new projects. The project has also established a network for those interested in getting involved in the arts – an art advisory group.

Is there another or follow on project planned?
Yes – a three year public art programme with more investment from partners.

How will this be funded?
Arts Council England, West Midlands, the private sector developer through planning gain, Optima Community Association and Birmingham City Council.

On a scale of 1-10, how would rate the success of the project for the organisation and the community (1 being poor, 10 being excellent)?
For the organisation 7, and for the community 6.

61

"Before this project the community lacked identity – everyone knows each other now."

Betty Boal, Treasurer

62

rekendyke art trail
south tyneside

Introduction

Rekendyke is located in the northern half of South Tyneside, on the bank of the River Tyne. In 1998 it had an estimated population of 7,180 and contained 3,840 households. Rekendyke ward showed high levels of unemployment (17.2% in September 1999), deprivation and possible social exclusion (P&R Policy & Research:2000).

Together, the William Sutton Trust and North British Housing Association own and manage 609 homes in Rekendyke, largely concentrated in a limited number of traditional low-rise terraced streets around Dean Road, Tyne Dock. In 2000 it was estimated that the turnover of these properties was around 20% per year, that properties were taking a long time to let

and there was increasing evidence of negative views developing among potential applicants and long-standing residents.

Revitalising Rekendyke was a regeneration project funded through the Single Regeneration Budget (SRB) challenge fund. The project was led by William Sutton Housing Trust in partnership with the local authority, North British Housing Association and local residents. Apart from improving the condition of the housing stock, the partnership's objectives were to address issues such as community safety, drug abuse, degeneration of the physical environment and low levels of economic activity.

"It's about the identity of the area."

**Nell Atkin, Rekendyke
Neighbourhood Initiative**

63

The arts project

At the beginning of the regeneration process a residents' group called Residents Reviving Rekendyke was constituted with the objective of promoting and improving the area, supported by the SRB partnership. The group wanted to run a project that would bring people together, enhance the environment and create a more positive identity for the area. Nell Atkin, the Community Development Worker for Rekendyke Neighbourhood Initiative, suggested an arts project. A steering group was set up which included local residents, housing association staff, the community arts officer and the head teacher from the local school. The group consulted local people and developed a proposal to design, create and install the Rekendyke Art Trail. The steering group applied for and obtained funding of £9,950 from the Northern Rock Foundation, £4,750

from the Coalfield's Regeneration Trust Community Chest and £4,050 in kind from Residents Reviving Rekendyke.

Residents were invited to an open meeting to shortlist artists for the project. Malcolm Smith was selected, and held a series of workshops to include residents in the design and creation of the work The enthusiasm and involvement of residents meant that 12 artworks were created instead of the four originally intended.

The project exceeded all expectations for staff and participants, creating a sense of community spirit and pride in the area, increasing involvement and making it far easier to get people to attend meetings.

"It's about the residents learning that they can take responsibility."

Jim Riddle, Vice Chair

64

"This project was used as part of the capacity building process and was excellent in what it achieved."

Nell Atkin, Community Development Worker

"Now there's more contact and friendliness in the community."

Jim Riddle, Vice Chair

Summary

Name of project
Rekendyke Art Trail.

Organisation
Residents Reviving Rekendyke.

Project leader
Original idea came from Nell Atkin and the project was led by the Residents Reviving Rekendyke Committee, which set up a steering group to manage the project.

Total cost of project
£18,750.

Length of project
19 months, from March 2001-Oct 2002.

How was the project funded?
£9,950 Northern Rock Foundation.
£4,750 Coalfields Regeneration Trust Community Chest.
£4,050 in kind from Residents Reviving Rekendyke.
£1,500 in kind from Groundwork.

How was it organised?
Residents and others volunteered for a committee who organised and supervised the project.

How was the community attracted to the project?
Initially through the resident's association and its steering group, who also worked with regeneration partners to help publicise the project more widely. 'Taster' workshops were advertised, posters were put up around the area, schools were petitioned, door knocking was carried out, children's workshops were held to try out ideas.

Who participated in the project?
Approximately 100 children and residents from the Residents Reviving Rekendyke area – all ages.

Was it a wider section of the community than would otherwise have been involved?
Yes, definitely – this project attracted a wide range of residents from the community – young and old.

What did the organisation expect to get out of the project?
The population had been particularly transient on the estate. The project was intended to facilitate involvement of the whole community, build and sustain community spirit and build bridges between different groups within the community. The partners believe these outcomes were successfully achieved.

What were the outcomes/outputs?
Twelve pieces of art were produced and displayed around the area, mostly installed on residents' houses. There was lots of involvement in the project by residents – it got them thinking about the area and its history. The area was rebranded positively. There was significant press coverage about the project and Rekendyke is now known locally as the area that has the art trail, rather than as an area where you would not want to live. It also led to a number of spin-off projects. For example, a reading project was planned for the following summer.

Were they the expected outcomes?
The outcomes and outputs were much more than expected. The original idea was to display four pieces of artwork – this grew quickly into twelve due to the response and involvement of the community.

Did the community learn any new skills from this project?
Yes – through shortlisting, interviewing and working with artists, organising workshops and managing a budget.

Was there a difference in the planned costs and final costs?
There was a £1,500 underspend, because Groundwork installed the art trail at no cost, and this has now been transferred to another community arts initiative, a quilting project.

Has it helped community engagement in other aspects of regeneration?

"I knew nothing about art before this project."

Betty Boal, Treasurer

People are friendlier, more interested in the area. Attendance at meetings has increased and residents are now more responsive to new ideas.

Is there another or follow on project planned?
Various other projects have been planned as a result, including a literature and a quilting project. Participants have developed more confidence to move on to other projects.

How will this be funded?
From the £1,500 left over from the Rekendyke Trail

project. Residents Reviving Rekendyke are now more confident about being able to attract funding from different pots of money for a variety of projects.

On a scale of 1-10, how would you rate the success of the project for the organisation and the community (1 being poor, 10 being excellent)?
10.

On a scale of 1-10 how would you rate the value for money aspect of the project ?
10 – excellent for what we got out of it.

"People in this area now have a pioneer spirit thanks to this project."

Frans Otto Novotny , Artist

tackling fear of crime through art
northmoor urban art project, manchester

68

Introduction

Northmoor is part of the Longsight area of South Manchester. The neighbourhood is made up of 1,400 properties – mostly street-fronting two-bedroom terraced houses in a 19th Century grid-iron pattern. Homes are of mixed tenure, with around 80% under private ownership. Manchester Methodist Housing Association owns and manages approximately 250 of the properties.

Northmoor suffered from high levels of poverty and multiple deprivation and in 1998 had around 200 empty homes. At this point it was declared a Housing Renewal Area and established within an Single Regeneration Budget (SRB) initiative. A vision for Northmoor was drawn up to provide a framework for regeneration of the area. This was based on extensive consultation with residents, who came from a wide variety of backgrounds and cultures. Local people said that they wanted:

- improvements in the physical environment
- improvements in community safety and
security, including measures to tackle burglary, traffic, street crime and fear of crime
- greater confidence, pride and ownership in the area
- people to know their neighbours, look out for and respect each other, and have a sense of responsibility
- local services and facilities for young people, families and older people

The regeneration programme involved over twenty different projects, all aimed at ensuring a more safe, secure, attractive environment, greater housing choice and a more sustainable community. The area was also the first of nine nationwide districts to pilot a Home Zone scheme in a regeneration area – a government funded scheme inspired by the Dutch 'woonerf' system. This aimed to create more of a 'courtyard' feel in residential streets by reducing the speed of traffic to an absolute minimum and enabling pedestrians to safely share space with cars.

The arts project

The BURA award-winning Northmoor Urban Arts Project (NUAP) was set up by a partnership including Manchester Housing, Manchester City Council Arts, Manchester Methodist Housing Association, the A6 Partnership and Northmoor Community Association. It aimed to encourage resident participation in some of the detailed design work that is a distinctive feature of the Home Zones. The regeneration partnership knew that it would be difficult engaging residents in the regeneration process, particularly when they are faced with the everyday problems of life. To try to make the process more meaningful, interesting and enjoyable, the partnership decided to commission community artists to work with residents and organisations in the area.

Artist Franz Novotny was selected to lead the project, after a process of shortlisting and presentations to the Northmoor Steering Group. A contract was agreed setting out the terms of the working relationship. He began to establish a programme of creative ventures that would bring positive benefits to the area, 'both physically and emotionally', many inspired by local residents. The following are some of the activities that helped the Northmoor Urban Arts Project obtain the British Urban Regeneration Association award for best practice in regeneration:

- a mini multiplex cinema was created in one of three empty two-up two-down properties
- another empty property was turned into the 'ImiTate'Gallery, where a number of local artists exhibited paintings
- a third property housed artists-in-residence during the programme
- artists were involved in the design of

J. RAI.

gateways, road surfaces, an underpass mural, and the bridge over Stockport Road linking Northmoor with green spaces
- artists worked with shopkeepers to improve shop fronts, and used boarded-up windows to display work
- support was given to local artists and creative businesses

A 2002 study of the most deprived wards in Manchester, Liverpool and London, sponsored by Help the Aged, demonstrated that 40% of older people had been the victim of crime in the previous two years, and that around a quarter of older people experienced intense social isolation and a lack of leisure activities in their area. These findings were noted by Northmoor Community Association, a registered company and charity that developed out of the local Residents' Association. They

acknowledged that there was little community activity for the over-50s in Northmoor, and felt that art classes might help them to interact, socialise and become more involved in the regeneration process.

Northmoor Urban Arts Project agreed to lead an additional project which aimed encourage older people to learn about the visual arts, create their own work and produce and curate their own local arts exhibition. Successful applications for funding were made by NUAP to the Arts Council's North West office (then called North West Arts Board) and to Age Concern.

The Community Association, local police and Neighbourhood Wardens identified older and vulnerable tenants who they felt would benefit from the project, and a participatory group was formed.The group took part in half-day workshops

"... the Northmoor Urban Arts Project has made a significant contribution to creating real community involvement in the area ..."

BURA's commentary on NUAP's award, November 2001

with professional artists where they were taught about colour theory, how to produce preliminary drawings and sketches, and various painting techniques. After each workshop, participants received support to overcome their fears of crime, and were given tips on community safety from key agencies working in the area. They were also taken to an exhibition at Manchester's City Art Gallery, an exhibition of their own work held at the Imi-Tate Galley, and a celebration party which encouraged wider community participation.

The project was successful in getting older members of the community out of their home and interacting with other community members. After the project,

one of the participants was inspired to set up a regular coffee morning to ensure that regular social activities could continue. Local support agencies and Neighbourhood Wardens now visit these sessions to enable ongoing dialogue with older residents in the area. The Women's Design Survey undertook a safety audit soon after the art project and said that they found it noticeably easier to engage this group of older residents than it would have been before the project. There was a marked reduction within the group of concerns and perceptions about the level of crime in the area. The publicity generated by the project and exhibition has helped to change perceptions of Longsight.

Summary

Name of project
Northmoor Urban Arts Project – Tackling Fear of
Crime Through Art.

Organisation
Northmoor Community Association and Northmoor
Urban Arts Project.

Project leader
Frans Otto Novotny, Artist.

Total cost of project
£5,095.

Length of project
3 Months, including 2 months planning.

How was the project funded?
Age Concern – £1,900.
Arts Council England, North West – £3,195.

Whose idea was the project?
It was the Community Association's idea. There was
nothing for older people in the area so they thought
art classes would help them to interact and socialise.

How was it organised?
Partnership was crucial. The Neighbourhood Renewal
Section helped the Community Association to apply
for funding. The project became part of the wider
Northmoor Community Arts Project. The artist, Frans
Otto Novotny, planned and ran the project.

How was the community attracted to the project?
Neighbourhood Wardens, the community policing
section and the Community Association identified
vulnerable tenants. It was part of a larger arts and
regeneration programme which aimed to build
confidence and trust. Door-knocking helped in
reaching the vulnerable and getting them involved.

Who participated in the project?
Eleven residents over 50 years old participated
directly in this element of the Northmoor Urban
Arts Project.

*Was it a wider section of the community than would
have otherwise would have been involved?*
Yes, definitely.

*What did the organisation expect to get out of the
project?*
The wider Northmoor Urban Arts Project aimed to
involve as many people as possible in the regeneration
of the area, including involving them in new
community activities. The painting workshops were
aimed specifically at older, more vulnerable residents,
and were intended to address their concerns about
crime and increase levels of social interaction.

What were the outcomes/outputs?
The participants produced various paintings and
there was an exhibition and celebration party
afterwards. This encouraged wide community
participation. The project was successful in getting
older people out of their homes, reducing social
isolation, engaging them in the regeneration process,
addressing fears about crime and putting them in
touch with local agencies who could advise on
community safety. It has also helped to change
people's perceptions of Longsight and we are now
trying to establish a permanent art gallery in
the area.

Were they the outcomes you expected?
Yes – the project exceeded expectations by bringing
the community together. It helped overcome the fear
of crime and was used as an opportunity to put local
people in touch with other agencies including the
Community Police Officer, energy team etc. It gave
the community confidence and introduced them to
some new services.

*Did the community learn any new skills from this
project?*
Absolutely. Apart from one participant, none of the
group had painted since they were at school. They
learned about colour theory, texture, scale transition,
painting, organisation, observation skills, art criticism,
lighting, exhibiting, developing an artistic language.
It also provoked new ideas.

72

"If we hadn't run the project people would have stayed at home and wouldn't have had the confidence to respond."

Frans Otto Novotny, Artist

73

Was there a difference in the planned costs and final costs?
No, they were on budget.

Has this project made a difference to community engagement in other aspects of regeneration?
Yes, definitely – this project has been successful in getting older members of the community out of their homes and interacting with others. Every one of the participants was sorry to see it end. There have been a lot of positive spin-offs. Regular coffee mornings are now held and there are far more social activities planned. Local agencies and Neighbourhood Wardens now visit these sessions to enable ongoing dialogue with older residents in the area. For example, the Women's Design Serviceis now doing a safety audit with women and through this project we have ready-made contacts.

Is there another or follow on project planned?
Yes – the safety audit for women. We are also trying to establish a more permanent art gallery in the area.

How will this be funded?
The Women's Design Service.

On a scale of 1-10, how would you rate the success of the project for the organisation and the community (1 being poor, 10 being excellent)?
8.

On a scale of 1-10, how would you rate the value for money aspect of the project ?
8 – lots of things have come out of it.

"I think that it has helped to make the community feel that they have ownership of the Foyer, which is an important project for the Isle of Wight."

Ian Darch, Foyer Manager

ryde foyer public art project
isle of wight

74

Introduction

The Isle of Wight Foyer, under the umbrella of Medina Housing Association, is considered one of the most important social projects on the Isle of Wight. Situated in George Street, Ryde, and opened in May 2000, it was designed to be a resource for the whole island. The Foyer provides good quality, affordable accommodation for 45 people aged between 16 and 25 who live on the Isle of Wight and are in housing need. Accommodation is provided for 6 months to 2 years. Each resident has a room with en-suite facilities, which are arranged in clusters of five sharing a kitchen and dining room.

The Foyer caters for a range of people, including those who temporarily need somewhere to live, people who are homeless and those who have behavioral problems. It is a holistic project that provides training in basic and social skills, healthy living courses, vocational courses and access to other training and employment opportunities. The Foyer has recently been awarded major grants from the New Opportunities Fund and the Department for Education and Skills. This has funded information technology and technical backup to allow the Foyer to provide up-to-date training in website design, music technology and video production. Take-up for this training has been high among Foyer residents, and there are plans to make it more widely available to non-residents, leading to the Foyer becoming a centre of excellence in these fields.

The centre aims to become part of community life, and is particularly looking to its on-site training centre to achieve this, by making courses available to the wider public. However, when the centre was first proposed there were strong concerns expressed by local residents and Barfield Resident's Association. To address this the Foyer Manager at that time, Ian Darch, conceived of a collaborative public art project that would engage both the young people and the resident's association. The aim was to change local pre-conceptions about the Foyer and anchor it in the community in which it is sited.

The arts project

The Island (SRB) Regeneration Partnership agreed to fund and lead the arts project and drew up an initial brief. The Foyer building would have two solid living and recreational areas connected by a glass atrium, which would also be the main entrance to the building. The atrium would extend to a height of five floors, with open walkways connecting the two sections of the building. It was felt that a project using glass as the medium would fit well with the overall design. A further grant was secured from Arts Council England South East (then called Southern Arts).

In order to interview and select artists, a steering group was set up that included Ian Darch, Foyer Manager; Sheila Potter, Barfield Resident's Association; Angela Norman, Youth Representative and Rachel Nightingale, Project Officer for the Island 2000 Trust. Short-listed artists were asked to give an informal presentation to the steering group, after which professional artist Sasha Ward was selected to lead the project. She would be responsible for planning the project, consulting with stakeholders, and then running workshops at which the glassworks would be made. The artist consulted the resident's

"I didn't know I could do it. Sasha showed me the techniques and I just created my own designs."

Charlie, Foyer resident.

76

association, the target youth group, the steering group and the architect. A plan was agreed which would result in eight glass pieces of art in the entrance door, designed and made by the artist and residents, and a large 20ft glass screen in the entrance hall.

The eight glass door panels were produced during a week of workshop sessions led by Sasha Ward and involving the resident's association, 12 young people from the Foyer and 12 pupils from Ryde High School. Participants worked together to create the overall composition, which was inspired by the landscape of the island, with each piece designed to link harmoniously with its neighbours.

The glass screen was made up of five panels of enamelled toughened safety glass. The intention was to suffuse colour throughout the building's entrance, and incorporate recognisable images inspired by Ryde and its architecture. The screen's images start with

buildings, rooftops and trees, then move upwards to the sea with its forts, boats, birds and distant shorelines. The 10mm thick glass was hand-painted with transparent and opaque enamels, sandblasted, fired and toughened.

The outcomes for the Foyer were positive in many ways. The artwork involved the wider community, including local people who did not live at the Foyer In doing so it raised awareness of the Foyer and increased support. The project involved people in the immediate vicinity in order to develop their recognition of the Foyer as a valuable community resource. One of the most vocal critics of the Foyer in its development stage is now one of its most avid supporters. Working with a local school provided the opportunity for pupils to learn new skills, and facilitated a sense of community ownership and increased involvement with the Foyer. The artwork has also vastly improved the physical environment of the Foyer.

*"We wanted the Foyer to have a bright modern look
and this artwork achieves that."*

Jacqui Hughes, Project Manager

Summary

Name of project
Ryde Foyer Public Art Project.

Organisation
Foyer For The Island, Medina Housing Association.

Project leader
Ian Darch, Foyer Manager and a sub-group of the SRB partnership, with Sasha Ward, Artist.

Total cost of project
£11,900.

Length of project
14 months.

How was th project funded?
£9,400 SRB bid submitted by the Isle of Wight Council and Medina Housing Association. £2,500 from Arts Council England (then Southern Arts).

Whose idea was the project?
Ian Darch, Foyer Manager.

How was the community attracted to the project?
Through the workshops, design process and the involvement of the resident's association and local school. The Foyer also held a number of events relating to the project, including an event to celebrate the unveiling of the artwork.

Who participated in the project?
12 pupils from Ryde High School (three are now resident in the Foyer), Barfield Resident's Association, 12 young people from the Foyer and Foyer staff.

Was it a wider section of the community than would otherwise have been involved?
Yes. The Residents' Association was originally against the Foyer. This project changed their perception of the young people who were going to be housed there, and helped ensure that consultation started before the Foyer was built. It also involved the wider community, including local young people. It's

doubtful whether any other type of activity would have achieved this outcome.

What did the organisation expect to get out of the project?
The organisation saw the project as a means of involving the wider community in developing a piece of artwork to enhance the physical environment of the Foyer.

What were the outcomes/outputs?
Eight pieces of painted glass in the entrance door and a 20ft glass screen, designed and made by the artist and residents. This has created a welcoming space for all visitors. Alongside this, the project has led to an increase in the skills of young people and local residents, and in local support and involvement in the Foyer.

The resident's association has six members on its committee aged between 50 and 80 years – a difficult group to get to interact with young people. The arts project helped to create a dialogue between the two age groups.

Were they the expected outcomes/outputs?
They exceeded all expectations. Ryde Foyer is particularly pleased with the extent that Foyer residents and others have respected the artwork.

Did the community learn any new skills from this project?
Yes, the young people learned a lot about art and design. One is now studying art at University as a direct result of this project, and others have gone on to take further education courses. This project, along with the music, web-design and video training, appear to have boosted the confidence, motivation and self-esteem of participants. It has also helped develop organisational and team-working skills.

Was there a difference in the planned costs and final costs?
The project was delivered within budget.

"It's been good for everyone who was involved and we have been left with a fantastic piece of art."

Jacqui Hughes, Project Manager

Has this project made a difference to community engagment in other aspects of regeneration?
Yes – it involved the community in the work of the Foyer and established community contacts for future liaison. The Foyer is now fully engaged with the community and this has helped residents integrate with the local community. The resident's association was born out of opposition to the Foyer but were won over through involvement in the arts project, which started before the building was erected. The resident's association now continues to assist and support Foyer residents.

Is there another or follow on project planned?
Not as ambitious, but as a result of this project , an arts and crafts course is included as part of the healthy living programme.

How will this be funded?
New Opportunities Fund.

On a scale of 1-10, how would you rate the success of the project for the organisation and the community (1 being poor, 10 being excellent)?
10 – as high as possible. It has been simply excellent.

On a scale of 1-10, how would you rate the value for money aspect of the project ?
10 – excellent value for money, particularly in relation to the cost of building the Foyer, which was £2.8m. The art project cost only £11,900.

"This collaboration between artists and residents is one way the Housing Action Trust brings artistic involvement to local communities across Liverpool, a key objective of our arts programme."

Sue Thomas, Director of Community Services, Liverpool HAT

80

further up in the air
sheil park, liverpool

Introduction

Liverpool Housing Action Trust (HAT) is a short-life government-sponsored body established under the 1988 Housing Act.It took over legal control of 5,337 homes in 67 tower blocks and 10 low-rise blocks from Liverpool City Council in October 1993, following a transfer vote by the tenants. It was given a mandate to operate until March 2005, and the task of redeveloping the housing stock and improving the environmental, social and economic conditions in the area. It would spend more than £260 million over its lifetime (about £20 million per year) on development and regeneration work. Of the 67 original tower blocks, 53 will have been demolished by 2005 to be replaced by low-rise housing. The Chair of the HAT Board was Paula Ridley OBE and the 10 other members (including four tenant representatives) were appointed by the Secretary of State.

Liverpool HAT adopted a Percent for Art policy, which meant that a percentage of the total budgets of all their developments would be spent on arts related projects.

The arts project

The arts project, which took place at the Linosa tower block in Sheil Park, provided a typical example of the way in which the Percent for Art budget was used. Two tower blocks had already been demolished and 154 new homes, a new community centre and a new health centre had been built in their place. Linosa's demolition was set for April 2004, to be replaced with 24 new homes. At 22 storeys, the Linosa tower block was Liverpool's highest building. The majority of its remaining tenants were retired and had lived in Linosa since it was first built.

The project was developed through the HAT's resident consultation structures, namely the Sheil Park Neighbourhood Panel. This met every six weeks to discuss local development, community development and housing issues with elected representatives from Sheil Park. The panel agreed a plan for the project. This would enable a range of artists practising in different mediums to work on-site, completely free of any fixed briefs, and to produce work that responded to the ongoing major development project the HAT was engaged in.

"This initiative has helped Liverpool HAT to develop a model of best practice for incorporating the work of artists in major housing-led regeneration projects. We have always believed that cultural activities play an important part in developing community identity, spirit and strength.

Paul Kelly, Liverpool HAT Community Manager

The project built on an earlier initiative called *Up In The Air* in which a small group of artists had worked with the residents of a nearby tower block that was due for demolition. The project was an attempt to get under the skin of the block and the community, to answer questions and explore people's experiences and expectations during the redevelopment process. Up In The Air had made use of empty flats as accommodation and studios for the artists. For Further Up In The Air, the concept was taken a stage further, with the flats used as key elements of the artwork itself.

In total, 25 artists took part, including painters, sculptors, new media and intervention artists. For a month at a time, six different artists would live in the tower block and at the end of that period there would be a three-day open exhibition for people to come and view the work. There were three residencies, held over a two-year period. Tenants were involved in interviewing and selecting artists from all over the country, including novelist and broadcaster Will Self who wrote a short story during his residency in the tower block. The first artist residencies took place in April 2002, the second phase in September 2002 and the final phase in April 2003. At the end of the third residency, work was documented and collated in a single publication which was launched in September 2003 in London, Manchester and Liverpool.

The workspaces in the blocks were open to residents, who were encouraged to get involved in the work as it developed, and participate in the book launch and exhibitions that followed. Some of the residents worked very closely with individual artists, which gave a great boost on both sides. For example, artist George Shaw was involved in the project and has seen his own profile increasing nationally. Many residents felt a real affinity with his work and a pride in the fact that he worked at Sheil Park, that he knows residents and gets on with them. The project received a great deal of media coverage including a full-page article in *The Observer* and six-page article in *Vogue Italia*. Residents' stories were used by a local writer, Jeff Young, as the basis of a broadcast Radio 3 play called Superblock. All this helped give a real confidence to Sheil Park residents.

Over 60 of the residents directly participated in the project in different ways, including visiting galleries, selecting the artists, organising private views, and hosting events in the blocks. Many more residents went along to see the work. The Housing Action Trust were impressed with the outcomes, stating that participating residents:

- demonstrated an ability and willingness to engage, debate and air their views
- gained an alternative perspective of the wider project
- gained confidence
- worked with each other and with artists, giving the community a boost
- gained an enhanced understanding of contemporary art

In addition, many more residents get involved in meetings than had done so before the project.

82

"Through this and other projects we have been an active partner and supporter of Liverpool's bid to be European Capital of Culture in 2008. Our aim now is to develop a co-ordinated approach between all housing providers within the city to this work, so that by 2008 there will be a wealth of projects and artists working with local communities in all parts of Liverpool. We see this goal as achievable."

Paul Kelly, Liverpool HAT Community Manager

"Such a ground breaking project would not have been possible had it not been for the vision and nerve shown by Liverpool HAT in supporting such an organic and open-ended project."

Leo Fitzmaurice, Neville Gabie, Artists/Curators

Summary

Name of project
Further Up In The Air.

Organisation
Liverpool Housing Action Trust.

Project leader
The project was managed by Paul Kelly of HAT's Community Development Department, in partnership with artists and curators, Leo Fitzmaurice and Neville Gabie, and the local neighbourhood panel.

Length of project
Two years.

How was the community attracted to the project?
Through involvement of the Sheil Park Neighbourhood Panel, which approved and helped supervise the project, and Sheil Park Residents' Association. HAT liaised with the Residents' Association on a day-to-day basis about issues as they arose. For example, the residents were involved in appointing a number of the artists from open submissions and, and HAT offered training to help them manage that process.

Who participated in the project?
25 local, regional, national and international artists, the residents of the high rise block and the surrounding community.

Was it a wider section of the community than would have otherwise been involved?
Yes – it enabled HAT to engage with residents who had not previously been involved in HAT's consultation structures, particularly men and young people.

What did HAT expect to get out of the project?
In broad terms there were very few expectations. HAT had hoped that the artists would enable staff and residents to look differently at this particular regeneration project, and for the personal elements – the impact on the lives of the residents – to be drawn out more clearly.

What were the outcomes/outputs?
The outputs of the artists were very varied. The work produced was of an exceptionally high standard, and the publication was a major piece of work created as a result of the project. Through the residencies, exhibitions and gallery visits, HAT was able to attract and involve new residents in their work. The project has made a huge difference to the community in terms of confidence. Firstly, it has gained national recognition, particularly in the arts world but also in

the regeneration context. It has made both staff and residents alike look differently at the wider scheme that they were delivering at Sheil Park. It gave the community a focal point around which they could work together on interesting projects and at the same time consider the wider development.

Did the community learn any skills from this new project?
Undoubtedly, yes, and not just the community, but also HAT staff and development workers. The major area of learning was around the whole issue of contemporary arts, other forms of art like new media, and the ability to engage in discussions, articulate their views about individual pieces (whether they liked them or not) and take part in visits to galleries. The community was very clear that through this project they had gained a new understanding of contemporary art and a real ability and willingness to engage, debate, and express their views.

Was there a difference in the planned costs and the final costs?
No, there were very fixed and generous fees for the artists. Each got a fixed budget for materials, and they all got the same, regardless of the medium. The book also had a fixed cost.

Has the project helped engage the community in other aspects of regeneration?
Emphatically yes. It has helped the community become stronger, new people have come out of the woodwork to get involved in the arts project and they have appeared at other HAT meetings and become involved in the development process. It has strengthened the community; more people have got involved in the community centre and community activities. There have been much more exciting activities including lots of visits to art galleries, visits to London – not just run of the mill local activities, and that's really drawn people together and created a social bond. Strong partnership working between staff and residents has also been developed.

Following this project, has it improved HAT's communication and interaction with the community?

Again, absolutely. There are strong structures in HAT to enable communication with residents, but there are often people who are intimidated coming along to meetings, working with architects etc. This project has enabled HAT to break down barriers and build stronger links with the community. There is still a long way to go, and there are still people who are hidden behind their doors, but the project meant that HAT has reached some new people.

Is there another, or follow on project planned, and how will this be funded?
HAT has successfully applied for £40,000 from Arts Council England to help to develop the project further. The idea is that – as the last residents move from the tower block into their new homes, and as the whole development project ends at Sheil Park – the focus for the artists moves onto the new estate, the new community and the new community centre. It is hoped that this will extend the arts initiative at Sheil Park for at least a further two-year period.

In addition, Sheil Park residents are involved in another arts project, through the Liverpool Biennial of Contemporary Arts, called Shrinking Cities. This project is linking four cities in different parts of the world, including Berlin and Brazil, and is exploring what happens when a city's population declines. The example of Sheil Park will be used as part of an exhibition at an art gallery in Berlin in October 2004.

On a scale of 1-10, how would you rate the success of the project, the organisation and the community (1 being poor, 10 being excellent)?
This has been the most exciting arts project for Liverpool HAT. It has broken new ground in terms of the approach that's been taken, and the openness of the brief for the artists, and it has used a genuine community development approach to community arts work. At the same time, the quality of the art produced has not been compromised. There have been some difficult pieces produced through this project, and the community and staff involved have been taken along with that. It is 10 for this project.

"I'm no Paxman or Kilroy, but I'm doing it."

Steve Thomas, Tenantspin presenter

86

superchannel the tower block
coronation court, liverpool

Introduction

The oldest tower block in Liverpool was Coronation Court in the north of the city. 10 floors high and containing 114 dwellings accessed by a labyrinth of corridors and stairwells, Coronation Court was an idiosyncratic design. Although it was considered by some to be ugly, cumbersome and inaccessible, sited some eight miles from the city centre, most of its tenants were passionate about their home. Its first tenants took up residency in 1956. In 2000 more that 70% of its tenants were over 60 years old, and 43% were over 70. When the Housing Action Trust first consulted about redevelopment of the block, one of the primary concerns of residents was keeping the community together. This provided the impetus for a partnership between the Foundation for Art and Creative Technology's (FACT) Collaboration Programme and HAT to create a media arts project with tenants.

The arts project

HAT and the Foundation for Art and Creative Technology (FACT) involved Coronation Court tenants in choosing artists to undertake the residency. Superflex, a collaboration of three Danish artists, were selected to lead a participatory media project called Superchannel and the Tower Block. The commission was managed by FACT's Collaboration Manager and HAT's Community Development Manager.

Superchannel was developed as a live TV channel on the Internet, broadcasting from a studio based in Coronation Court. Superflex had developed software which allowed video (live or taped) and sound to be sent at the same time as a live text. This meant that the online public could interact with the producers and tenants via the real-time chat function and exchange ideas.

The aims of the commission were:

- to explore the potential for Superchannel to become a focal point for discussions about the block
- to develop and express community identity at Coronation Court

"After all, not everyone wants to sit in a meeting in order to have their say."

Catherine Simmons, Resident Participation Manager, Liverpool

- to involve tenants from Coronation Court in directing the project, and in research, production and performance
- to introduce tenants and HAT staff to new creative technology and its use within the arts field
- to encourage the development of a critical understanding of art and its processes among HAT tenants and staff
- to promote the inclusion of tenants in a major exhibition within the city – Video Positive 2000
- to introduce artists with an international reputation to the community
- to promote resident participation in regeneration and social housing issues through constructive debate and the sharing of experiences

Superchannel succeeded in involving tenants in producing shows about their lives, their homes and their community for global broadcast. These ranged from debates about the future of high-rise living to online campaigns for tenant rights or local dances. An internet-based television studio was established in a community flat within Coronation Court, and broadcast content as part of Video Positive Arts Festival 2000 in Liverpool. It was featured in an exhibition in the Bluecoat Art Gallery in Liverpool, and a publication about the project was produced. Superchannel gave tenants a set of new media tools with which to maintain and develop their community links and influence decision-making about their future.

The initial project involved the direct participation of ten residents of the block (population of 80) in the

production process. Of these, six were new participants in the work of Liverpool HAT and had not previously been involved in other consultation structures.

So successful was Superchannel that HAT and FACT worked together to get each of Liverpool's remaining tower blocks onto the web, so that the Coronation Court project became just one community within a larger online community. The result was Tenantspin, one of 26 global superchannels. This was served by a webcasting studio, managed by and for tenants of Liverpool HAT, and located within Liverpool's new £10million purpose built arts centre, the FACT Centre in Wood Street.

Launched in March 2001, Tenantspin webcast hour-long shows once a week which looked at issues such as:

- rent increases
- resident participation and technology
- landlords
- demolitions
- the built environment
- high rise living
- regeneration
- public and community art
- 21st century homes

Tenantspin was managed by a steering committee comprising 12 tenant group members and representatives from FACT and HAT.

88

"Everything that you see on Tenantspin has been developed, produced and promoted by tenants. That means research, camerawork, computer operation, publicity, presentation, training and studio management."

Paul Kelly, Community Development Manager, Liverpool HAT

"60% of Liverpool HAT residents are over 65 years of age, the vast majority over 70 and 50% are disabled or have a long-term illness. Tenantspin offers them an alternative way to participate and also challenges perceptions of older people and technology. Residents are in control of Tenantspin – its content and direction."

Catherine Simmons, Resident Participation Manager, Liverpool HAT

Summary

Name of project
Superchannel the Tower Block.

Organisation
Liverpool Housing Action Trust (HAT), in partnership with the Foundation for Art and Creative Technology (FACT).

Project leader
FACT's Collaboration Manager and HAT's Community Development Manager.

Length of project
1 year – April 2000 to March 2001.

How was the community attracted to participate in it?
HAT worked closely with Coronation Court's Resident's Association and neighbourhood panel in planning and managing the community's involvement. FACT involved the resident's association in all decisions relating to the training and the content of broadcasts. Many of the residents were attracted by an interest in the technology, and went on to become involved in other HAT activities. Many of the older residents were also attracted by a personal interest in learning how to use the internet.

Who participated in the project?
The project was targeted at residents of Coronation Court; there was a core group of approximately 10 residents who were involved in the project.

Was it a wider section of the community than would have otherwise been involved?
On a small scale it was. In a tower block of around 80 residents, four or five new people became engaged with HAT as a result.

What did the organisation expect to get out of the project?
This was very much a first arts project for Liverpool HAT and the aim was to explore how a participative project using new media and technology could develop within a tower block setting. Coronation Court was an unusual design, and members of the community were particularly isolated from each other. It was hoped that this project would re-invigorate community spirit within the tower block.

What were the outcomes?
The profile of the tower block was raised, and the issue of community involvement was promoted more widely across the city. Four or five new residents became involved with HAT. It enabled more direct engagement with people living in the block, and a better understanding of their feelings and concerns about the regeneration programme. All shows made were saved and are archived on the internet.

Were the outcomes expected?
HAT wasn't sure how many people would engage at Coronation Court. They had been engaging with less than 10% of the community at the time the project was initiated, and it really was an opportunity to try something completely different.

90

"As a major regeneration project there is plenty of opportunity in HAT for residents to participate in decisions, from setting rents to designing new homes. Whilst HAT relies upon traditional approaches to resident participation through the representative tenant body – the High Rise Tenant Group – both HRTG and HAT see Tenantspin as an alternative way to involve residents."

Catherine Simmons, Resident Participation Manager,Liverpool

91

Did the community learn any new skills from this new project?
Participants learned new computer, broadcast and internet skills.

Was there a difference in the planned costs and the final costs?
No, it was a very fixed budget.

Has this project made a difference to the community and its engagement in other aspects of regeneration?
This was a community where individuals had become very isolated from each other. The project went some way to help to develop a sense of community, and in that regard it made a difference. Some of the residents became very good friends and continued to develop the project as it took on a new guise in the city centre context, and they have stayed involved.

However, HAT does not make any great claims that the project transformed the Coronation Court community. Following the project, HAT admitted that it was still difficult to engage the community in other aspects of regeneration, but they did get four or five new people involved, so it strengthened community representation. The greater impact of the project came when it was taken forward as Tenantspin across other HAT sites, linked to a city centre location, which has really engaged the community.

Is there another, or follow on project planned and if so, how will this be funded?
Yes, Superchannel was a short lived project. Since then it has evolved into Tenantspin, funded by a range of arts organisations, BT, and Innovation into Action, through the Housing Corporation, and has become very successful.

On a scale of 1-10, how would you rate the success of the project for the organisation and the community (1 being poor, 10 being excellent)?
6 or 7 for Superchannel in terms of success, but it started what became Tenantspin and that has been a hugely successful project.

*"It has raised aspirations and guided people
to a possible career in the arts."*

Trevor Evans, Project Leader

got what it takes
castle vale, birmingham

Introduction

Castle Vale lies six miles north-east of central Birmingham and is the city's largest 1960s-built housing estate. It comprises 3,786 homes with 10,000 residents in an area covering 1.5 square miles. The estate was formerly managed by Birmingham City Council but was transferred to Castle Vale Housing Action Trust after a tenant/leaseholder ballot in 1993. Over the last 10 years the Housing Action Trust has spent nearly £300 million on regenerating the estate.

The Housing Action Trust (HAT) has promoted arts activities as a way of ensuring that all sections of the community are involved in the regeneration process. From the outset they believed that by encouraging all sections of the community to participate in and enjoy arts and leisure activities, pride and self-esteem would be generated within the community, contributing strongly to the process of regeneration.

HAT developed an ambitious arts strategy which has supported the ArtSite programme, bringing international artists to the estate, and an artist-in-residence scheme, which has led to a number of public art pieces including the Sentinel sculpture by Tim Tolkein. It has also supported Vale FM, a community radio station first piloted in 1996, which has since gone from strength to strength and is now virtually self-supporting. It runs from a state-of-the art base in one of only two tower blocks not due for demolition. Vale FM runs two 28-day broadcasts a year, alongside a number of training programmes, and provides a valuable resource to the community.

Castle Vale now enjoys an unprecedented interest and participation in the arts, which has started to impact positively on the image of the estate and boosted participation in the regeneration process. In 1998 a Community Arts Development Officer was appointed to further develop the arts strategy and outreach work. The success of the outreach work led to the emergence and support of resident-led arts organisations, which have been putting on and promoting their own polished and well-attended performances. Got What it Takes is an example of one of these outreach projects.

"My son has been involved in this scheme, he has gained great confidence and is also getting involved in more schemes. I think this is great and would like to see this going further."

Mr R Edwards, Resident

93

The arts project

Got What It Takes began in October 1999 as a 12-month project funded by a Millennium Commission grant of £2,765. Local resident Trevor Evans conceived of the idea as a means to engage young people in arts activities *"that would not put them in the firing line for criticism from their peer group"*. This meant the activity needed to be of excellent quality, contemporary, relevant to the lives of young people, and able to work around them and their commitments.

Participants were attracted to the project by posters, leaflets, a website, and through word-of-mouth

recommendation. The initial intention of the project was to work with young people from the Castle Vale area in forming a number of musical acts and to conclude in a performance. However it became much more than this.

The first production by the Got What It Takes team took place in August 2000 at Castle Vale Community Leisure Centre. The performance was a play, *Camp Blood*, and featuring a cast of nine young people. More than 150 people attended the event including the local MP Robin Corbett and Housing Action Trust Chairman Richard Temple-Cox. The project was so

"We planned the project and community involvement came with it."

Trevor Evans, Project Leader

well-supported and received that the group were inspired to develop it into a youth music and theatre organisation.

In August 2001 Got What it Takes held its first ever summer school, Summer Rampage. The idea of this summer school was to enable both new and existing members to produce a show for performance after an intensive two week rehearsal period. Of the 19 participants, just under a half had never performed on stage before. All of the participants were included in the cast of Teenage Jungle Rampage which was performed to an audience of around 300 people. Both the performance and the summer school were hailed a success and have become annual events.

Got What it Takes also provided opportunities for instrumentalists and vocalists to produce music in a range of styles and perform at different venues. For example, Flashman Burns are a band who have been part of Got What it Takes since its outset, and it has enabled them to take part in a number of high profile events – including National Lottery Fun Fest in Birmingham City Centre, which saw the band supporting Darius Danesh of Pop Idol. The organisation has been able to draw down funds to purchase around £2,000 worth of music equipment, which has helped groups like Flashman Burns to rehearse and perform using top-of the range

equipment. More recently, Got What it Takes has been collaborating with Vale FM to encourage young people into broadcasting. For example, Live and Laughing, a two hour long show, was written, produced and presented by Got What it Takes members and broadcast to Castle Vale residents.

Got What it Takes has developed participants skills in communication, team-working, organisation, time management, performance, music, technology, composition, scenery and production. The project has raised the aspirations of young people, guiding some to possible careers in the arts as well as developing transferable skills. Trevor Evans, the original inspiration for the project, is now employed full-time as a music and drama instructor at Castle Vale School and has become a board member at HAT and a recognised community leader.

In 2002, Got What it Takes developed its own Performing Arts Leaders Scheme (PALS) which was designed around young peoples interest in performing arts and intended to develop their leadership skills, not only in the arts but also in wider activities affecting young people and their community. It has inspired participants to respect themselves and others, and helped teach them how to make their voices heard and how to listen to others.

94

95

"I have enjoyed the show and I wasn't aware that there was so much talent here in Castle Vale. Trevor Evans has done exceedingly well."

Sandi Evans, Resident

Participants were attracted to the project by posters, leaflets, a website, and through word-of-mouth recommendation.

Summary

Name of project
Got What It Takes.

Organisation
Castle Vale Housing Action Trust.

Project leader
Trevor Evans.

Total cost of project
Originally £2,765 and then £1,000 per performance.

Length of project
Ongoing since 1999.

How was the project funded?
Original £2,765 Millennium Award, and ongoing support from HAT's arts programme.

Whose idea was the project?
Trevor Evans.

How long did it take to plan?
3 months.

How was the community attracted to it?
Through posters, the website and leaflets but mainly word of mouth.It was seen as an independent project that was not controlled or censored by HAT.

Who participated in the project?
11-16 year-old residents, with 20-108 people in the cast at any one time, and 400 participants in total.

Was it a wider section of the community than would have otherwise would have been involved?
Yes, definitely, as it was fresh and exciting and appealed to the age group the organisers wanted to attract.

What did the organisers expect to get out of the project?
The organisers expected to put on a performance of an original script *Camp Blood* written by the cast and artist involved.

What were the outcomes/outputs?
Initially two performances were put on over a two-month period. 150 people turned up for the first performance and more than double that for the second one.

Were they the expected outcomes?
In terms of numbers – less than expected, but in terms of quality it exceeded expectations.

Did the community learn any new skills from this project?
Yes, drama, music, composition, scene change,

"We put on two performances over a two month period,150 people turned up for the first performance and more than double that for the second one."

Trevor Evans

97

performance skills, working together, organisational skills and time management.

Was there a difference in the planned costs and final costs?
Yes, the initial project was £300 under budget.

Has this project made a difference to the community?
It has provided young people with a choice of creative activities and helped develop their skills. Due to its continuing success it has grown each year It has raised aspirations and guided people to a possible career in the arts. It has improved communication and interaction with the community.

Is there another or follow on project planned?
Yes – further work with music groups and bands is planned.

How will this be funded?
Through the school, leisure centre and other community groups who buy into the project.

On a scale of 1-10, how would you rate the success of the project for the organisation and the community (1 being poor, 10 being excellent)?
9 – very successful, new and exciting and growing each year.

On a scale of 1-10, how would you rate the value for money aspect of the project?
10 – excellent. The project operates on a small budget and at no cost to participants.

"The scheme also aims to enable tenants to establish self-worth and self-esteem and to recognise individual strengths and promote self-development."

Jane Sillis, Arts Manager

goldhawk road garden
look ahead housing and care

Introduction

Look Ahead supports vulnerable adults and young people, by providing housing and other support services that help them to lead independent lives. Look Ahead service users include people experiencing mental illness, people with learning disabilities and homeless young people, adults and familes. Look Ahead gives support to more than 3,000 vulnerable people across London and the South East.

Look Ahead's corporate aims are:

* to reduce the number of rough sleepers on the streets
* use innovative solutions to increase options for tenants and residents
* encourage service user involvement
* recognise, value and develop strategies to support diversity
* develop quality services through continuous improvement
* build strategic partnerships, alliances and collaboration

Look Ahead's Annual Report 2004 describes the vulnerable it supports as follows:
* 22% were under 18 years old

* 24% were 18-25 years old
* 52% were 26-59 years old
* 46% were British/European
* 28% were African
* 7% were Black British Caribbean
* 5% Asian

Look Ahead's Arts Programme
For the last decade Look Ahead has carried out innovative arts projects as part of the support it offers to vulnerable people.

The aims of the arts programme are to:

* encourage service user involvement
* enable service users to become more integrated into local communities
* help improve the home environments of service users
* interface with Look Ahead's other services such as training, employment, development and maintenance

In 1999 Look Ahead appointed a professional Arts Manager and in 2000 Look Ahead's Board adopted an arts strategy, which actively informs Look Ahead's

98

... the garden project created a positive setting for service users and staff to develop relationships soon after tenants moved in.

arts programme. An independent evaluation by Phyllida Shaw in 2003, supported by the Arts Council England, London found that Look Ahead used the arts very effectively to deliver its core aims.

"The Look Ahead arts programme is an example of 'joined up thinking' in action. Housing professionals are working with artists to create opportunities for service users and staff that are rare in the housing sector." Phyllida Shaw, 2003

The arts programme at Look Ahead's Aldgate Hostel, is cited as an example of good practice in the 1999 DCMS PAT 10 report on using the arts to combat social exclusion.

Look Ahead's arts programme comprises public art commissions, which involve consultation and participation with service users, staff and local residents and participatory arts projects with service users and staff. Many of Look Ahead's arts projects are carried out in partnership with arts partners such as the Whitechapel Gallery, Museum of London, Tate Modern, Serpentine Gallery, Photographers' Gallery and local authority arts teams. Goldhawk Road Garden is the first of two examples of successful projects undertaken through Look Ahead's arts programme featured in this guide.

The arts project

Goldhawk Road Garden – Look Ahead Housing and Care, London Borough of Hammersmith and Fulham.

Introduction

352-354 Goldhawk Road is a new development which opened in summer 2002 and provides housing and support services for 16 people aged 18-65 who have a history of rough sleeping and have severe or enduring mental health problems. In association with this, the tenants may have a dual diagnosis (substance misuse). The scheme is situated in the London Borough of Hammersmith and Fulham and has been developed by Look Ahead in partnership with the borough and the government's Rough Sleepers Unit.

The scheme is staffed 24 hours a day providing the residents with a supportive environment in which they can increase their life skills in order that they can eventually move on to independent living. The scheme also aims to enable tenants to establish self-worth and self-esteem and to recognise individual strengths and promote self-development. Artist Elizabeth-Jane Grose and LB Landscape Architecture created a garden with Look Ahead service users for their new home from November 2002 to September 2003. Participants who have mental health, drug and alcohol issues were involved in every stage of the design, creation and maintenance of the garden. Service users participated in practical workshops with the artist, landscape architect and gardener designing the garden and then creating aspects of it including a formal herb garden, woven hazel hedge and wild meadow. An average of five service users took part in 18 sessions over 10 months. Staff were impressed by the level of service users engagement, their commitment to the garden project and the positive affect it had on participants confidence and self-esteem. The garden was opened in September 2003 by the Rt Hon Estelle Morris MP, Minister for the Arts. The project was funded by the King's Fund, Look Ahead Housing and Care, CRASH, its supporter

The Story of Christmas Appeal and its patrons Hanson, B&Q and Aggregate Industries.

The objectives of garden project were:

- to create a residential garden at Look Ahead's project for vulnerable people at Goldhawk Road, London
- to involve staff and service users in key decisions about the design of the garden and of the artworks it contained
- to involve staff and service users in the achievable aspects of creating the garden
- to encourage staff and service users to maintain parts of the completed garden

The opening celebrated service users' achievements with everyone who had been involved in the project; decision-makers and Look Ahead's peers in housing, care and the arts. The event challenged negative stereotypes of vulnerable people. Service users created an attractive garden on previously undeveloped land, they report that it is calm and up-lifting to be in the garden and look at it from their flats. The creation of the garden provided a positive environment for staff and service users to work together. One service user has taken a huge interest in planting and taking care of the garden and helped with the recruitment of a gardener. He feels that the garden project has changed his life for the better and staff agree that he has grown in confidence and self-esteem as a result of his involvement in it.

As well as taking care of the garden with the help of regular visits from a gardener, service users set up an arts group. The arts group has already taken part in a project with other Look Ahead service users at the Whitechapel Art Gallery recording music and stories on a CD.

One service user has taken a huge interest in planting and taking care of the garden and helped with the recruitment of a gardener ...

101

... he feels that the garden project has changed his life for the better and staff agree that he has grown in confidence and self-esteem as a result of his involvement in it.

Summary

Name of project
Goldhawk Road Garden.

Name of organisation
Look Ahead Housing and Care.

Project leader
Jane Sillis, Arts Manager.

Cost of project
Cash cost £48,520.

Length of project
2 years 3 months (including planning and fundraising).

How was the project funded?
£31,000 King's Fund.
£10,000 CRASH and its supporter the Story of Christmas Appeal.
£1,800 help in kind from the patrons of CRASH – Hanson, B&Q and Aggregate Industries.
£7,520 Look Ahead Housing and Care.

Whose ideas was the project?
It was a collective idea, which initially came out of discussion in summer 2001 with the project architects Prior Manton Tuke Powell, Look Ahead housing, care and development staff and the Arts Manager. Ideas were further developed with the Arts Manger and staff at Goldhawk Road when the scheme opened in spring 2002 and with service users as they moved in over spring and summer 2002. Goldhawk Road staff were involved in the selection of the artist and landscape architect. Service users and staff were active in all subsequent decisions and plans for the project.

How long did it take to plan?
1 year and 4 months including fund raising.

How was it organised?
The project was overseen by a project co-ordinator who was supported by the Arts Manager. An artist, community gardener and landscape architect worked with care staff during workshops to design, plan and make the garden. LB Landscape Architecture oversaw the building of the hard landscape by contractors Visible Changes.

How did organisers attract the community to it?
The community was attracted in various ways:

- discussion about the garden project at service users meetings
- posters in the project, advertising discussion and practical sessions with the artist and landscape architect
- staff knocking on service users' doors when practical sessions with the artist and gardener were taking place, which encouraged service users to attend individual key work sessions
- service users joining in sessions in the garden and the common room when they saw other people participating
- a service user helping with the recruitment of the two gardeners who have worked on project.

Who participated in the project?
Service users and staff at Goldhawk Road.

Was it a wider section of the community than would otherwise have been involved?
Staff were very impressed by service users engagement and participation in the project, these were higher and more consistent than they anticipated.

What did the organisers expect to get out of the project?
The creation of an attractive communal space on an undeveloped site.

What were the outcomes/outputs?
As above. Also, vulnerable service users made decisions about their home environment, developed confidence, self esteem and life skills. Service users

have continued to take responsibility for the care of the garden.

Were they what the organisers expected?
These match the projects original project aims.

Did the community learn any new skills from this project?
Budgeting, design, teamwork, decision making, planting and garden maintenance.

How was the community involvement planned?
Service user involvement was the principal focus of the project. Service users were invited to take part in practical sessions in which the garden was designed, planned and created, these were supported by the artist, landscape architect, gardener, project co-ordiantor and care staff. Service users were encouraged to participate in parts of the project which were achievable. The hard landscaping and specialist work was undertaken by contractors.

Who planned and ran the project?
The project was planned and overseen by Look Ahead's Arts Manager with the project co-ordinator. LB Landscape Architecture oversaw the contractor, Visible Changes and the landscape work. The project manager for Goldhawk Road and his team supported the artist, gardener, project co-ordinator and landscape architect.

Was there a difference in the planned costs and the final costs?
Yes.

Was this more or less than expected?
The project cost £17,520 more than originally estimated. Unforeseen work had to be done to prepare the site, which cost £7,520 and these costs were met by Look Ahead. It cost £10,000 more than anticipated for the hard landscape work to be completed and these costs were met with an additional grant from CRASH and the Story of Christmas Appeal.

Has this project made a difference to the community?
Yes, the project has created an attractive communal space which service users and staff enjoy looking at and being in. Individual service users have grown in confidence and self-esteem. Staff and service users are committed to taking care of the garden and are funding a gardener who they will work with through tenants' service charge. Service users feel positive about their home environment, enjoy being in it and taking care of it. The garden project triggered the forming of an art group, which has taken part in a project with the Whitechapel Art Gallery.

Following this project, has communication and interaction with the community improved?
Yes, the garden project created a positive setting for service users and staff to develop relationships soon after tenants moved in. Individual service users have grown in self-esteem and confidence.

Is there another or follow on project planned?
The garden project is ongoing with a gardener visiting the project regularly to work with service users in the garden.

How will this be funded?
Service users have agreed to pay for a gardener and to restock the garden from their service charge.

On a scale of 1-10, how would you rate the success of the project for the organisation and the community (1 being poor, 10 being excellent)?
9 – very positive for the organisation.

On a scale of 1-10, how would you rate the value of the money aspect of the project for the organisation and the community?
10 – Look Ahead drew in £41,000 to the scheme and a further £1,800 help in kind. We have received a further £2,000 for an irrigation system from CRASH.

103

"Rainforest Walk scheme is a new project for vulnerable young people, which opened in 2004 and provides homes for 20 homeless 16-25 year-olds."

Jane Sillis, Arts Manager

rainforest walk
look ahead housing and care, bracknell forest bc

Introduction

The Rainforest Walk scheme is a new project for vulnerable young people, which opened in 2004 and provides homes for 20 homeless 16-25 year-olds. Our service users have become homeless for a variety of reasons; they may, for example, be care leavers. Service users are given support to develop life skills, to access training, education and employment and to move on to independent lives.

Local residents had expressed concern about a new project for vulnerable young people in their neighbourhood. Look Ahead had used arts projects very successfully in Tower Hamlets to help build positive relationships between homeless people at Aldgate Hostel and the local community. Look Ahead invited Fox Hill Primary School, neighbouring the new project in Rainforest Walk, and the chair of the local residents group to help select an artist for a public art commission for the new building at Rainforest Walk. The school also hosted a residency by the artist and architects.

The arts project

Artist Esther Rolinson worked with architects Prior Manton Tuke Powell designing a light work for the new building, Rainforest Walk. The aims of the art commission were:

- to create an interesting and attractive building with links to the neighbouring built environment
- to create an art commission as part of the building

Its objectives were:

- for the artist and architects to collaborate on the design of the building
- for the school, community members and architects to be involved in the selection of an artist for the commission
- for the artist and architects to undertake a residency at Fox Hill Primary School
- for drawings of the building and of the commission to be publicly displayed in Bracknell
- for the artist to design a work for the building which will be built and manufactured by specialist contractors

The artist and architects undertook a four day residency at Fox Hill Primary School in November 2002 working with 36 Year 5 students and the art co-ordinator. The aims of the residency which linked with art, design and citizenship in the National Curriculum were:

Look Ahead invited Fox Hill Primary School, neighbouring the new project in Rainforest Walk, and the chair of the local residents group to help select an artist for a public art commission for the new building at Rainforest Walk. The school also hosted a residency by the artist and architect.

106

- to visualise the new building
- to consider how an artwork may be integral to the building
- to further the pupils understanding of how an artist/architect develops work
- to further pupils understanding of the people who will live in the building
- to explore the idea of home and neighbourhood as well as learning more about how buildings and public art works are designed and constructed.

The planned practical outcomes were:

- notes and brainstorm sheets of ideas
- photographs of important features
- light experiment models
- elevation sketches
- 3D models

Students' works was presented by the artist, architects and Arts Manager at a residents consultation meeting in November 2002. Residents were very positive that students and staff had shared their ideas so actively with the artist and architects. The school pupils chose to name the new road where the Look Ahead project was built, Rainforest Walk. They celebrated the unveiling of the new road name in July 2003, which was covered by the local press.

The artist further developed her design for a light work for the building drawing on ideas she gained while visiting the site, working with students and with the architects. The artist's designs were displayed at an open day for local residents at Rainforest Walk in March 2004 before service users moved in. The artwork - 'Air Wave' - an acrylic and light work was installed in May, 2004.

Young people at Rainforest Walk became part of an active art group and took part in an arts project at South Hill Park Arts Centre in spring 2005.

Summary

Name of project
Rainforest Walk.

Name of organisation
Look Ahead Housing and Care.

Project leader
Jane Sillis, Arts Manager.

Cost of project
£58,800.

Length of project
2 years five months including fundraising and planning.

107

Students and staff explored the idea of neighbourhood and community and what makes some members of communities vulnerable and in need of support.

How was the project funded?
£44,800 Arts Council England, South East.
£12,000 Look Ahead Housing and Care.
£2,000 Prior Manton Tuke Powell, help in kind from project architects.

Whose idea was the project?
The project was developed by Look Ahead's Arts Manager, development and housing and care staff with the project architect Prior Manton Tuke Powell. The idea for the project was developed with Christine Mitchell, head teacher and Gaynor Griffiths, art co-ordinator at Fox Hill Primary School and with Alec Hines the chair of the residents group who helped with the artists' interviews. Fox Hill Primary School co-planned and hosted the artist's and architects' residency at the school.

How long did it take to plan?
1 year.

How was it organised?
The artists' selection was organised by the Arts Manager with the support of a public art consultant Hazel Colquhoun. The artists and architects residency at Fox Hill Primary School was planned and co-ordinated by artist Esther Rolinson and Gaynor Griffiths, art co-ordinator with architects Christina Larrington and Peter Manton, Prior Manton Tuke Powell.

The public art commission was organised by the artist with the Arts Manager. Specialist help in the design, manufacture, construction, installation and light of the artwork and the design of the landscape was provided by:

- Anthony Hayes, structural engineer, Michael Barclay Partnership
- Martyn Love, manufacturer, Camberley Signs
- Theo Paradise, lighting designer, Sutton Vane Associates
- Jane Banks, landscape architect, LB Landscape Architecture

How was the community attracted to the project?
The Arts Manager contacted Fox Hill School and the chair of the local residents group, inviting them to interview three short listed artists for the residency and commission in May 2002. Local residents were invited by Bracknell Forest BC to the consultation meeting in November 2002. Look Ahead invited residents to a pre-opening event in March 2004.

Who participated in the project?
The chair of the local residents group, head teacher and art co-ordinator at Fox Hill Primary School took part in the artists' interviews with the architect, Look Ahead staff and a public art consultant. 36 Year 5 students at Fox Hill Primary School, the head teacher and art co-ordinator took part in the artists' and architects' residency in November 2002. Local residents attended a consultation meeting in November 2002.

Was it a wider section of the community than would otherwise have been involved?
The organisers chose to work with a target group in the community, students and staff at Fox Hill School.

What did the organisation expect to get out of the project?

- for students and staff at Fox Hill Primary School to develop a clearer understanding of the young people moving in to the project at Rainforest Walk
- for students and staff to learn about the design of the building and of the public art commission and to be actively involved in the process
- to start to develop a positive relationship between Look Ahead, staff and children at Fox Hill Primary School and with local residents which could be further developed when young people and staff moved into Rainforest Walk.

What were the outcomes/outputs?

- students and staff at Fox Hill Primary School have begun to develop a positive relationship with Look Ahead. This was an excellent foundation for developing friendly relationships with the project at Rainforest Walk now staff and service users have moved in
- the artist and architect undertook a residency at Fox Hill Primary School which enriched the National Curriculum
- students and staff discussed the design of the building and the public art commission with the artist and the architects. This began to develop a sense of ownership of the new building outside of their school
- local residents who were concerned about the opening of a new project for vulnerable people in their neighbourhood were able to focus on a positive aspect of the project. This helped to develop residents' confidence and goodwill towards the project at Rainforest Walk
- the lightwork has made a positive contribution to the new building in Rainforest Walk and to the neighbourhood.

Were they what the organisers expected?
Yes.

Did the community lean any new skills from this project?
Students learnt about the design of a building and of a public art commissions. They developed model making, drawing skills and thought conceptually. Students and staff explored the idea of neighbourhood and community and what makes some members of communities vulnerable and in need of support.

Who planned and ran the project?
The interviews were planned and run by the Arts Manager with Look Ahead staff.
The residency was planned and run by the Arts Manager, artist and Fox Hill Primary School staff. The residents consultation was planned and run by Bracknell BC with Look Ahead. The art commission was planned and run by the artist with the Arts Manager with specialist support.

Was there a difference in the planned costs and the final costs?
The landscape work costs more than was estimated.

How has this project made a difference to the community?
By starting a positive relationship between local residents and the project at Rainforest Walk – in particular with Fox Hill Primary School.

Following this project, has it been easier to engage the community in other aspects of regeneration?
Yes.

Following this project , has communication and interaction with the community improved?
Yes.

109

Is there another or follow on project planned?
See above.

How will this be funded?
Funding has been secured from the Paul Hamlyn Foundation for the project with South Hill Park arts centre.

On a scale of 1-10, how would you rate the success of the project for the organisation and the community (1 being poor, 10 being excellent)?
8 – the organisation only worked with a selected part of the community but this was positive.

On a scale of 1-10 how would you rate the value of the money aspect of the project for the organisation and the community?
10 – the commission drew in a grant of £44,800 which has enabled Look Ahead to fund a major public art commission, an artist and architects' residency.

conclusion

choosing and delivering suitable arts projects for an area or neighbourhood

Introduction

This guide illustrates the wide range of arts activities that can be supported by housing associations, developers and resident groups. Some of these aim to deliver long-term physical improvements to the appearance and design of buildings and public spaces. Others are focused on providing participatory activities to increase community cohesion and quality of life for residents, or engage them in consultation about changes to their neighbourhood.

As illustrated in this guide, projects can involve a variety of mediums and art forms, including music, dance, drama, festivals, literature, oral histories, documentary, and visual arts such as sculpture, crafts, film, photography and multi-media. The way in which projects are delivered also varies, and might include artist-in-residence programmes, workshops and training, artist-led consultations, organised visits to cultural venues, community-based performances and exhibitions, participatory volunteer programmes, and commissions of new work.

Deciding upon a suitable project for a particular neighbourhood will require a responsiveness to the context and issues affecting that community. However, there are some general principles which can be applied across all types of project to help ensure effectiveness and quality of delivery. The following section offers guidance on each of the key stages in choosing and delivering an arts project in a community setting.

Identifying partners, stakeholders and their roles

An early step in any project is to identify key stakeholders and partners and their various roles. Consultation with potential partners at an early stage can help give direction to a project. Partnerships can also help in planning the intended legacy of a project, and ensuring its benefits are sustained in the longer term.

The local community will always be a key stakeholder, and project planning should be done in an open way to involve as many local people as possible. This can be helped by inviting representatives from local residents' associations or community networks to get involved in the project's management group. In addition, consideration should be given to involving local schools, colleges, businesses, faith groups, cultural organisations based in the area, and community support services and agencies. Other key stakeholders are likely to be the housing association, landlord or developer, and the local authority.

Partners should seek to develop a clear understanding about their various roles in delivering the project, and what resources each can contribute. Resources might include staff time, spaces, equipment, skills and management expertise.

Agreeing the aims and objectives of a project

Partners can often have different expectations and priorities, and it is important to discuss and reach agreement on the main aims of a project at its inception. Having a clear and shared understanding of the primary objectives of a project will make it easier to agree a project plan, brief and evaluation framework.

In deciding upon a project's objectives, consideration should be given to whether the arts activity is intended to tackle a specific issue affecting the local community. While all types of participatory arts projects have the potential to enhance community cohesion and increase resident participation, many projects are also designed to address specific problems or developments in the local community. These might include:

- consulting with residents who are reluctant to be involved in the more formal consultative structures (eg I Love My Little Flat, Further up in the Air, Superchannel, Neighbourhood Watching)
- encouraging the young or unemployed into training, employment and community involvement (eg Newbold, Got What it Takes)
- reducing crime and anti-social behaviour (eg Pembroke Street, Tackling the Fear of Crime through Art)
- improving understanding and cohesion between culturally diverse residents (eg Newbold Project and Tenants in Focus)
- improving the image of an area, developing a sense of community identity and pride, and attracting and retaining residents (eg Rekendyke, Images of Newbold)
- improving the quality of people's lives and increasing community cohesion

through individual and collective creativity (eg All Saints Playground, Pembroke Street, Closer, Goldhawk Road)

- helping communities deal with major regeneration or change programmes by supporting communications and helping express residents' views (eg Further Up In The Air, Superchannel)

An awareness of the wider context, including the social and demographic profile of the local community, will inform a project's aims and objectives. Are there particular target groups, which it has been hard to reach, or that it is important to involve? These might include minority ethnic groups, older residents or young people at risk of exclusion. What are the cultural traditions and background of different sections of the community? Arts activities are more likely to be effective if they can engage with the interests and experiences of local people. Community consultation before commissioning a project can help identify these interests (see section below on 'involving the community') and can inform the selection of an artist. Alternatively, the brief can be framed in such a way that the artist takes a lead role in engaging with the community and developing a project that is responsive to local culture and environment.

Another factor might be the existence of any refurbishment, re-design or new build activities taking place in the area. Refurbishment and new build schemes offer a time-limited chance to embed art commissions into a wider programme of physical changes, and can help deliver integrated improvements to the liveability and image of an estate. New developments can also offer an important source of finance for arts projects through Section 106 or Percent for Art agreements.

Many projects involve temporary or permanent changes to public spaces and buildings. These might be freestanding commissions or 'integrated' artworks, involving the design of street furniture, buildings or lighting (eg Rekendyke Art Trail, Tenants in Focus, Ryde Foyer Public Art Project, Pembroke Street, Goldhawk Road Garden and Rainforest Walk). This type of project offers a means of engaging with residents, while creating a sense of ownership in the visual identity of their physical environment, and a lasting legacy of improvements.

Stand-alone public art pieces can be commissioned for almost any public area, but a consideration of how the piece will work alongside other design elements is critical. Freestanding commissions can add distinctive landmark elements to a space and give it a more prominent identity. These might include large scale stand alone sculpture; artist designed structures, shelters or viewing platforms; 'gateway' artworks visible upon entering the area; environmental sculptures which utilise the power of wind, sun or water, and light sculptures or installations.
Preparation for commissioning such projects is likely to require a technical specification of the site, and consultation with planners and architects. The location of pieces will also need to thought through to accommodate any future access by utility companies.

113

"As a result of this project I am now going to adult learning to learn more about digital editing – it has definitely opened doors for us."

Mary Hayes, participant

"This project is featured on the local BBC website."

Brian Morgan, artist

"We are always looking for new opportunities to engage with our tenants and provide opportunities for them to learn new skills."

Elaine Ballard, Chief Executive, Taff Housing

With larger scale refurbishment or new-build projects, engaging an artist to work with the planning team from an early stage can be beneficial. Not only can artists assist in managing the consultation with residents. They can also work in collaboration with architects and planners to inform the design of anything from railings, gates, paving surfaces and windows to tiling, brickwork, lighting, signage and street furniture. Their involvement can help create a more coherent and distinctive overall visual identity for public spaces.

Planning, costing and managing the project

The next stage is to draw up a project plan and budget, and agree roles and responsibilities for each stage of managing the project. Agreement should be reached on who will act as the commissioning agency, who will manage the budget, submit applications, participate in the selection process etc.

If a resident or local community group is leading the project and applying for funding, it will need to establish an identity for the group if it does not already have one. This will involve adopting a constitution and opening a bank account with two different signatories. Set up a simple logo and strap line, such as 'working with the community', and elect a small committee to oversee the operation and finance of the project. Being well-organised helps give funders confidence in the group and the project. Asking a local dignitary to support the aims of the group can also help – someone recognised in the local community such as Iman, vicar, MP, local councillor or businessman.

Whether the lead organisation is a community group or housing association, they will need to form a management group or steering committee to oversee delivery of the project. Where there is no-one on the management group with experience of managing community arts projects, or with specific arts expertise, it will usually be necessary to contract an agency or consultant with the relevant experience. Commissioning a feasibility study can also help identify different options for and likely costs of the project in advance. There may be funding available to support this feasibility work.

In most cases it will be necessary to identify an individual who can take lead responsibility for project management. A project manager can be appointed at the outset of the commission, either from in-house staff or an external consultant. The cost of the project management will not normally exceed 15% of the total budget. The project manager can take the project through some or all of the following stages:

- feasibility and brief
- selection and appointment of artist(s), including drawing up contracts
- developing consultation frameworks
- overseeing delivery and financial management
- obtaining any relevant permissions, insurance and licenses

- documentation and exhibition of work in progress
- liaison with partners and external bodies
- publicity
- evaluation

Before agreeing a budget, consideration should be given as to what communal resources and facilities are available for use by artists and residents. Are there existing local community spaces suitable for workshops, performances or exhibitions? If not, is there a need to make new spaces available (eg Closer, Northmoor Urban Arts Project and I Love My Little Flat) or build partnerships to provide these (eg Superchannel and Tenantspin).

Developing the budget will involve detailing each element of income and expenditure. Income is likely to come from both 'cash' and 'in kind' investments, and the latter will include the estimated value of volunteers time. Obtain written estimates wherever possible, to avoid disputes at a later stage, and ensure that estimates include any VAT or setting up costs.In devising the budget, make sure that all costs are covered. The following provides a checklist of some of the likely costs:

- feasibility and research, including the costs of artists' design proposals
- recruitment and advertising costs
- artists fees, travel, subsistence and expenses
- project management fees
- materials, fabrication and installation costs
- community outreach programme costs
- insurance and licensing (permission of Parks, Highways and Licensing departments of the local authority might be needed if the project involves activities or installations in public spaces)
- hire of equipment and venues
- marketing, including design, print and distribution of publicity materials
- overheads such as telephone calls, postage, electricity and gas
- safety equipment and clothing if appropriate
- delivery and storage costs
- celebratory or launch event costs
- evaluation and monitoring
- maintenance

It is important to make sure that there are appropriate fees in place for artists. This will help in recruiting artists with appropriate skills and experience, and ensuring that the work is of a high quality. It will also be a condition of funding from some partners. Arts Council England produces a guidance note: *How to Pay Artists* (2004) available from:

www.artscouncil.org.uk/documents/information/phpsX7mV3.doc
or through their information line on 0845 300 620.

117

The management or steering group should meet regularly (usually monthly) to discuss and monitor the budget and prevent overspending. Keep funding partners, the community and other stakeholders informed with regular updates.

Selecting an artist or group of artists with the appropriate skills to work with community groups

The process of selecting an artist for a project is usually overseen by a selection panel made up of the main partners and community representatives. It may be necessary to supplement the panel with external expertise eg site architects or professionals with experience of commissioning artists. It is suggested that artistic expertise is always represented within selection panels.

The selection panel will draw up and agree a brief for the work, which should clearly outline the following:

- the background and wider context for the project
- who is commissioning the work
- the vision and aims of the commission
- the role of the artist, including any role in consultation
- site details and technical briefs where appropriate
- available resources, budget and fee
- ownership and copyright issues
- maintenance issues, durability, and health and safety
- the timetable and contract stages
- the selection process
- the artist's requirements in responding to the brief

Further advice on drawing up a brief, with examples, can be found at: www.publicartonline.org.uk

As a general rule, avoid making the brief too prescriptive, in order to encourage imaginative and varied proposals from artists.

There are a number of possible approaches to recruiting an artist – an open or limited design competition, competitive interview or direct appointment. Where the contract exceeds £10,000, an open tendering process will usually be necessary. There are a range of options for advertising the brief.

If it is considered important to involve local artists in the project it may not be necessary to look far, as many artists live in council and housing association properties. Try the local press or even residents association newsletters. The Neighbourhood Watching project demonstrated successful outcomes by engaging local artists through the residents' association.

An advert in specialist national and international arts press such as *Arts Professional* will reach a wider pool of potential applicants. The arts department of the local authority will usually have access to relevant databases and networks of artists. The regional office of Arts Council England may also be able to offer advice and assistance in advertising the brief, and provide contacts for local commissioning agencies.

Local cultural organisations and specialist arts colleges in the area can also assist with recruitment. The Pembroke Street project took advantage of the fact that the then Plymouth College of Art and Design was running a HND course in Design Metals, and were able to take on the contract with an artist for design and fabrication of the panels, gates and fencing.

On appointment, a contract should be drawn up with the successful applicant. This should clearly set out the terms of the appointment in relation to each of the areas covered by the brief (see above). It should also deal with matters relating to intellectual copyright and ownership of the artwork on completion of the project. Sustainability, insurance and maintenance issues can also be addressed in the contract. For example, the client could stipulate that the artist provides a full maintenance schedule for the work, or produces replacement 'spare parts' which can be kept in storage by the owner or official maintenance body.

Ensuring all sections of the community are engaged

Ensuring a sense of local ownership and engagement by the community is usually critical to the success of any community arts project. There are a number of ways of achieving this.

Adequate community consultation from the beginning of a project can mean that the setting up phase will be slower, but the activities which follow are more likely to be embedded, relevant and sustainable. Consultation can be timetabled to coincide with other important events or meetings such as architects' presentations, building openings, or community festivals and celebrations. Consultation can take a variety of forms including:

- meetings with key players
- slide presentations of artists work
- exhibitions, informal and formal discussions
- site visits to other projects
- temporary projects as a precursor to a permanent commission
- workshops with artists

Accessible premises are very important to encourage local people to see arts projects as something that they can become involved in. Try to identify suitable premises which can serve as a base and showcase for the project.

Allow the management of the project to be as transparent as possible, with open meetings to encourage a broad range of new people to get involved. Avoid the perception that a small, closed group are leading the project, which can lead to resentment and being labelled a 'clique'. Multiple entry points such as courses, events, tasters etc can facilitate wider access to a project.

Some ethnic and religious groups may prefer meetings or workshops at particular times taking into account, for instance, prayer times. Women attending workshops on their own may also be an issue. Women-only workshops might help attract those who would not normally attend mixed sessions.

Develop a marketing and communication strategy to help keep people informed at every stage of a project, and increase levels of participation. Communication tools used by the case studies included posters, flyers, press releases, letters, door-knocking, public meetings, presentations at faith groups, local press and media, and radio and online networks.

Regular progress reports including photographs, publicity and quotes will help keep people feeling involved, and can be distributed with resident newsletters. Always provide clear instructions for residents to get in touch with queries or feedback.

Evaluating projects

Evaluation can often be forgotten or seen as an additional burden imposed by funders. However, evaluation should be seen as a vital element of any project in that it provides a way of measuring its success from both the participants' and funders' perspectives. An effective evalution strategy will usually be planned and embedded in a project from its beginning. It can help:

- ensure that resources are used effectively
- measure delivery against aims and objectives
- provide evidence of impact
- set standards and ensure quality control
- give a voice to participants and residents
- provide information about the projects strengths and weaknesses
- make the case for future projects or further funding

In order to be effective, an evaluation system should be designed to directly relate back to the original objectives. Where possible, it should also be flexible enough to capture unexpected outcomes and benefits.

When evaluating the project, a multi-perspective approach will provide the most comprehensive assessment of the impact. The key stakeholders will normally be:

- past and current participants
- user groups

- trainees
- staff
- artists
- partner agencies
- funders
- contractors
- architects

The diversity of arts projects in terms of both their objectives and methods makes a standardised and comparable approach to evaluation difficult. Most of the case studies in this handbook have employed a mixture of quantitative and qualitative evaluation using various methodologies. Arts Council England publishes a useful Guide to Evaluating Arts Education Projects which has transferable lessons for community arts projects. Hard outcomes or outputs are generally easier to measure than the soft outcomes (eg the impact on people's confidence or sense of community cohesion). The latter will normally require more in depth surveys or interviews.

Specific examples of the type of measurable 'hard' data collected includes:

- works of art produced/number of shows/concerts
- expenditure and levered investment
- workshops run
- number of participants
- audience/visitor numbers
- skills obtained by participants
- follow on courses or jobs obtained by participants
- staff involved
- publicity generated
- follow on funding/spin-offs

121

Evaluation might also seek to establish some of the less quantifiable outcomes such as the impact on individuals' personal development and social networks. Evaluation frameworks might include questions in the following areas:

- self esteem/self respect/self-confidence
- attitudes towards place eg sense of belonging
- attitudes towards getting involved
- skills and knowledge
- behaviour eg trying new things
- trust in others
- standards of behaviour
- people looking out for each other (reciprocity)
- social networks and connections
- levels of participation in community organisations and events
- learning about other peoples' cultures

Questions relating to people's attitudes, behaviour and perceptions on the above can be asked, for example, three months prior to commencement of a project and then three months after completion of the project to establish any evidence of change.

Evidence should be collected from all stakeholders. For instance housing association staff/partner agencies can be asked over time whether the project assisted in changing normal perceptions of the area.

Evaluation can be carried out using the following methods:

- a video diary kept of the project may be a way of assessing soft outcomes
- questionnaires could be sent out to a random sample of past / current participants
- group interviews
- one-to-one interviews held with individual participants and agencies
- telephone and door-to-door surveys
- consultant brought in to shadow the artist through the process

Housing association staff involvement in the evaluation is a good way for them to become more widely known in the area, find out what people think and generate enthusiasm. If there is a thorny conflict surrounding the project, it may be better for an outsider to talk about the project with local people and find out what the shades of opinion are. Familiar members of the community are more likely to understand how people feel and know how to gain access to them.

For questionnaire design and analysis, if your organisation does not have relevant expertise, we recommend teaming up with someone who can help such as your local college or university.

Accessing funding

Community arts projects are not necessarily expensive. Housing associations and resident groups are often able to support projects through core budgets, and most partner funders will look for this as evidence of the commitment of partners, and the longer-term sustainability of arts initiatives. Innovative and ambitious projects can also lever match-funding from a variety of sources.

The featured case studies were funded as follows:

- Arts Council England
- National Lottery Awards For All
- Single Regeneration Budget
- Estate Action funding
- landlord or housing association contribution
- tenant's association contribution
- Housing Corporation, Community Training and Enabling Grant

122

- SureStart
- business sponsorship (ie Lloyds TSB, B&Q, Ibstock Bricks, Cream)
- from the Housing Association, Local Authority or developers' capital costs, through Section 106 or Percent for Art agreements
- architects' donation
- local authority contribution from regeneration, arts, leisure, education or community development budgets
- ticket sales and donations
- Northern Rock Foundation
- Coalfields Regeneration Trust Community Chest
- Age Concern
- Neighborhood Renewal Fund
- Millennium Commission award
- New Opportunities Fund award
- Kings Fund

Locally specific regeneration funding received by some organisations featured in the case studies is no longer applicable. Also, the Millenium Commission and New Opportunities Fund have now become the Big Lottery Fund. The section below provides an updated guide to the main sources of public and charitable funding.

In accessing funding for a project, it can be a good idea to begin with smaller applications before moving on to larger grants. A £5,000 Awards for All grant is an ideal place to start for new groups.

123

The Arts Council's *Guide to Alternative Funding Opportunities* provides a useful source of information about other funding sources. Other helpful online resources include:

- Fundfinder – a registered charity that produces software to help individuals and not for profit organisations to source funding opportunities www.fundfinder.org.uk
- The Arts Funding Guide – a comprehensive source of funding for arts www.dsc.org.uk
- Voluntary Arts Network – provides information on funding in its regular briefings and you can join an e-mail list to receive regular updates including funding information. www.voluntaryarts.org.uk

Government funding

Arts Council England and the Arts Council of Wales
These are the national funding bodies for the arts in England and Wales and are responsible for distributing public money from Government and the National Lottery. Information about the current objectives and priorities of each Council can be found along with application forms and guidance for downloading on the Arts Council England website at www.artscouncil.org.uk or the Arts Council of Wales website at www.artswales.org.

Local authorities

Local authorities are the second largest supporter of the arts in England after the Arts Council. They play a central role in supporting the arts locally, not only through direct funding of arts organisations and events, but also through the provision and management of arts venues, the promotion of arts events, and advice and support services delivered through their arts officers. Local authority funding of the arts is discretionary: they are able to support the arts but it is not a statutory requirement.

All local authorities operate differently, with their own structures, policies, grant-in-aid criteria and schemes. In most councils there is an arts or culture department that has prime responsibility for the support and funding of the arts. In some councils however, other departments – eg tourism, education, regeneration, housing or planning – acknowledge the value of the arts to their sectors by providing additional funding or support for artists and art organisations in the area.

Section 106 – Planning gain

Section 106 of the Town & Country Planning Act 1990 allows a local Planning Authority (LPA) to enter into a legally binding agreement (planning obligation) with a land developer to contribute towards the costs of a facility or project of benefit to the local community. The obligation is sometimes termed as a 'Section 106 Agreement'. Developers' contributions are secured by means of the planning agreement and can fund new public art commissions, community arts facilities and buildings, or activities – either on the site being developed, or in an area nearby. Access to Section 106 funding is often strengthened by the existence of a Percent for Art policy adopted by the local authority. Where such a policy exists, a minimum of 1% of agreed capital costs for new build, refurbishment, landscape and demolition expenditure is usually earmarked for artists' involvement or community arts activities.

The Section 106 route would normally be pursued as a source of finance where there is a significant new capital project (10 or more housing units) planned in the area.The developer's contribution to arts projects will usually be negotiated as part of a package of benefits. However, there are also local authority-wide community benefits that can be met from planning obligations which can result in pooled Percent for Art funds being held by the local authority. Contacting your local authority arts or planning department is a good place to start.

Funding from other government departments

There are currently a number of government initiatives focused on promoting active communities and tackling major social problems such as high crime and poor health, which acknowledge the role the arts can play in helping them to achieve the aims. They provide some funding for arts projects that address social issues and work with socially excluded groups. You should be aware however, that the work is locally specific and so the level of funding available for arts activities depends upon where you are based, and the priorities within that specific area.

Four current key initiatives are:

- Neighbourhood Renewal fund (NRF), which aims to improve public services in the 88 most deprived local authorities in England in order to narrow the gap between these areas and the rest of the country

- New Deal for Communities (NDC), a community based intensive regeneration programme, which is taking place in some of the most deprived neighbourhoods in England

- Positive Activities for Young People, a nationwide scheme that involves young people at high risk of social exclusion in voluntary supporting and cultural activities during school holidays and out of school hours. This is managed by local Connexions services

- Children's Fund, which focuses on developing services to ensure that those children and young people most at risk of social exclusion are identified early and given the necessary support to overcome disadvantage and achieve their potential

- To find out about the above initiatives go to: www.governmentfunding.org.uk

Community Training and Enabling (CTE)

The Housing Corporation provides grant funding to help housing association residents explore ways of being more involved in decisions about their housing through its Community Training and Enabling programme. South Liverpool Housing were awarded CTE funding for the Closer project featured in this guide. The Closer project's key aim was to increase resident participation within the regeneration of Speke and Garston by encouraging people to take a stake in their wider environment.

The programme will help housing associations and their residents to:

- develop better ways of giving residents more control of their housing – for example, in the provision of services, in decision making, and in trying out new ways of doing things
- get residents involved more effectively in regeneration and investment projects
- support initiatives for residents to be involved in strategy, community, planning, and partnerships

125

- develop links with other sources of finance for communities such as neighbourhood management.

The programme can also help groups of residents to receive grants directly from the Corporation for projects that support the policies outlined in the Housing Corporation publication, Communities in Control as long as the projects are for activities that will improve the services their housing association normally provides. You can visit www.communitiestakingcontrol.org for project ideas.

What could the grants cover?

The Housing Corporation wants the grants to help residents examine, review and influence the options for their housing and communities more deeply than is commonly accepted today. In addition, as residents' needs are different in every case, other activities could qualify and they welcome suggestions on what these might be. As residents may be concerned about more than just their housing, a grant could be part of a package that includes other sources of money to deliver wide-ranging improvements, for instance regeneration or employment grants.

Housing associations are already expected to provide funds to help their residents become involved in managing their homes. CTE grants are to pay for something more – working on a new idea or a different way of doing things.

Associations should already be carrying out their normal involvement of residents and providing them with the resources to be involved. If a CTE proposal is being put forward, the Corporation expect associations to work with and support its residents in drawing up the project, especially where it is resident-led. If necessary, associations should also help residents to be involved in building partnerships with other organisations.

Who can apply?

Both associations and residents groups can apply for funding directly or through agents, who could be the association or another organisation. Where residents groups apply, they should show that they have systems in place to manage the money effectively. This will usually be a bank account, arrangements for signing cheques and paying money, and for accounting for income and expenditure.

Where can you find out more?

More details and downloadable application forms are available on the website: www.housingcorp.gov.uk under Community Training and Enabling. Otherwise each of the Corporation's local offices can send you an information.

National Lottery

Awards For All

Awards for All is aimed at local communities and funds projects that enable people to take part in arts, sports, heritage and community activities, as well as projects that promote education, the environment and health in the local community. The application process is designed to be short and simple and applicants are told if they are successful within 12 weeks.

Who Can Apply?

- not-for-profit groups
- parish or town councils, schools or health bodies
- people who can use the grant within one year

Awards cannot be given to individuals. Predominantly residents and community groups are awarded funding from Awards For All, though Housing Associations are not specifically excluded. Currently you can apply for grants between £500 and £5,000. To build on its ongoing success and make it even easier for local communities to benefit from lottery funding, the Government is proposing to double the current upper limit of the Awards for All (England) programme to £10,000 from April 2005. The programme will continue to be a light touch scheme with a single application and a fast turnaround. There is also a proposal for an easy access grant of up to £500. Awards For All in Wales will be considered separately.

Applicants are asked how their project will meet the aims of Awards for All:

- extending access and participation
- increasing skill and creativity
- improving the quality of life

How to apply

You will need to fill in an application form, which is available from the application telephone line, the website www.awardsforall.org.uk or the regional offices. You can apply at anytime and there are no deadlines.

The Big Lottery Fund

The Big Lottery Fund is a new organisation that will hand out half the money for good causes from the National Lottery. It was created by merging the New Opportunities Fund and the Community Fund.

One of its first main funding programmes to be launched is the Young People's Fund, which aims to support projects to improve local communities and offer more opportunities to young people to achieve the following:

127

- being healthy: enjoying good physical and mental health; living a healthy lifestyle (eg football training, cookery classes, support from peers)
- staying safe: being protected from harm and neglect; growing up able to look after yourself (eg after-school clubs, self-defence groups, sexual health advice)
- enjoying and achieving: getting the most out of life; developing skills for adulthood (eg theatre groups and role-play, learning digital music, writing resume classes)
- making a positive contribution: giving back to the local community and society; not offending or behaving anti-socially (eg recycling programmes, creative arts club, 'clean up your park' schemes)
- economic well-being: overcoming socio-economic disadvantages to achieve full potential in life (eg helping homeless young people live independently, exam support)

There are three types of grant available under the Young People's Fund:

- grants to individual young people (or small groups of young people) to help them make a difference in their communities
- grants to voluntary and community organisations to run local projects with and for young people
- grants to voluntary organisations to fund national projects

The Big Lottery Fund is also continuing to give support to other types of community project previously funded through the New Opportunities Fund and Community Fund. To find out more visit the website at: www.biglotteryfund.org.uk or call 0845 4 102030.

Trusts and Foundations

This is by no means a comprehensive list of trusts and foundations that provide funding for arts projects. What is included here represents a very small selection of major UK trusts. The association of charitable foundations website contains useful tips on how to apply for funds and a list of charitable organisations: www.acf.org.uk

Paul Hamlyn Foundation, www.phf.org.uk
- supports arts initiatives in all parts of the UK that address inequality of access and lack of opportunity to experience and enjoy the arts
- grants of £5,000 to £100,000
- grants available to organisations with a charitable purpose

Clore Duffield Foundation, www.cloreduffield.org.uk
- supports arts, education, arts and museum education, health and social welfare
- particularly interested in supporting children, young people and society's

most vulnerable individuals
* only funds registered charities.

W A Cadbury Trust, www.wa-cadbury.org.uk
* supports arts music and drama projects, social welfare and community and self help groups
* grants available to charitable groups in Birmingham and West Midlands only
* grants range from £100 to £5,000

Wates Foundation, www.watesfoundation.org.uk
* supports community capacity building for disadvantaged groups, promotion of citizenship values, spiritual well being and understanding in society. Also supports culture, environmental and heritage projects
* grants up to £25,000 available to charitable groups
* London and South East only

Ragdoll Foundation, www.ragdollfoundation.org.uk
* promotes the development of children through the arts
* preference will be given to applications, which will apply to young children during their early years (0-8 years of age)
* grants available from £500-£20,000

The Ernest Cook Trust, www.ernestcooktrust.org.uk
* the trustees are particularly interested in applications, which provide opportunities for young people to gain qualifications; to further their employment prospects or assist training in crafts that are in danger of dying out
* trustees concentrate on educational aspects, which include arts crafts and architecture
* grants available from £100-£3,000
* charitable organisations may apply
* bias towards rurally situated projects

The Kings Fund, www.kingsfund.org.uk
Small grants (London only) are given to support the setting up of new health projects targeting disadvantaged groups, or to encourage the exploration and sharing of new ideas in the health field, via publications, conferences and networking. The biggest grant under this scheme is £5,000, but most grants are for much less than the maximum

The Kings Fund prioritise applications that:
* increase equity and justice; tackle inequalities in health
* promote racial and cultural diversity in health
* encourage public, user and patient involvement
* promote better work across organisational and professional boundaries

The Small Grants programme is aimed particularly at:

- small and new voluntary organisations and community organisations
- specific small-scale health projects relating to the priority themes
- sponsorship of events/publications and other activities that aim to promote debate, spread ideas and share good practice relating to the priority themes

Applications will only be considered from voluntary organisations with an annual income of less than £250,000. Applicants will need to enclose a copy of their organisation's most recent accounts to demonstrate that they meet this criterion.

Northern Rock Foundation, www.nr-foundation.org.uk
For projects located in the North East of England. The primary aim of this grants programme is to help disadvantaged people due to:

- age, eg young people and old people
- disability
- displacement eg refugees, asylum seekers, survivors of domestic violence
- the collapse of industry or other employment providers
- geography – where people live may affect their ability to get basic services, to work together for mutual benefit or to enjoy a healthy and fulfilled life
- prejudice and discrimination, for example, against gay men and lesbians or black and minority ethnic people

They prefer to assist by responding to peoples' own views of what needs to be done and equipping them, financially, to make changes themselves. Grants are available for amounts up to and over £15,000.

The Prince's Trust, www.princes-trust.org.uk
The Prince's Trust helps groups of young people aged 18-30 who want help to undertake training, run projects in their communities or start up in business.They have various schemes supporting arts activities and creative businesses. An example is Nueva Generacion, a troupe of young dancers from Latin American countries, which grew out of a project funded by the Princes Trust to run workshops for young Latin American refugees and migrants in England.

Funding arrangements for groups are currently changing, and can vary from one region to another. Check website for details or make contact with your regional office.

Business Donations or Sponsorship

You may be able to obtain arts funding from private companies in the form of sponsorship and charitable donations. Charitable donations come from a company's charitable budget which is subject to tax benefits, but a company making a charitable donation is not allowed to make commercial gain from their donation.

Sponsorship is different, with the money coming from a company's advertising or marketing budget. You will not get sponsorship unless you are offering the company something, ie corporate image publicity etc. This sponsorship could be in the form of money or in kind support eg from a DIY store donating materials. It is generally easiest to gain sponsorship from businesses located near to the proposed arts project.

To find a company who may be willing to sponsor a project in the area of arts activity, obtain the local business directory produced by the Chamber of Commerce www.britishchambers.org.uk. It may also be worthwhile looking at:

- The Major Companies Guide
- A Guide to Company Giving
- The Hollis Sponsorship and Donations Yearbook
- Arts and Business (www.aandb.org.uk)

Also take a look in the *Yellow Pages* for local companies and the local paper to see what companies have sponsored art projects in the past and may be willing to do again in the future.

Bibliography

Arts Council, 2004. *The Impact of the Arts*. Arts Council

Bell, R. Falk, I.,1998. *Groups of Groups: The Role of Group Learning in Building Social Capital* Centre for Research and Learning in Regional Australia

Blake Stevenson Ltd, 2000. *The Role of the Arts in Regeneration.* Scottish Executive Central Research Unit: Edinburgh

Cap Gemini Ernst & Young, 2003. *Delivering summer activities in high crime neighbourhoods: the intensive evaluation of Splash Extra 2002*. NOF

Carey, P & Sutton S, 2002. Closer: *An Evaluation of a Community Arts and Regeneration Initiative.* Liverpool John Moores University

Caswell, G & Lewis B, 2001. *Creative Solutions: The Use of the Arts in Regeneration*. Bolton Metropolitan Council

Coalter, F, 2001. *Realising the Potential: the Case for Cultural Services – The Arts*. Local Government Association. Published online <www.lga.gov.uk> in late 2001

Coleman, J, 1988. *Social Capital in the Creation of Human Capital*, American Journal of Sociology. (94) Supplement 95-120

Collier, P, 1998. *Social Capital and Poverty*. Social Capital Initiative, Working Paper Number 4

DCMS (a), 2001. C*reative Industries Mapping Document*, Department of Culture, Media and Sport

DCMS (b), 2001. *Culture and Creativity: The Next Ten Years*. Green Paper, Department of Culture, Media and Sport

DCMS, 1999. *Report of the Policy Action Team 10, Arts and Sport*, Department of Culture, Media and Sport

DETR, 2000. *National Indices of Multiple Deprivation*. Office of National Statistics

Earthy, S. Maltby, S. Arber, S. Cooper, H. 2000. *The Use of Cognitive Interviewing to Develop Questions on Social Capital for the 2000/2001 General Household Survey.* Office For National Statistics

Etzioni, A, 1993. *The Spirit of Community*. New York Crown Publishers

Falk, I. & Harrison L, 1998. *Indicators of Social Capital: Social Capital as the Product of Local Interactive Learning Processes*. Centre for Research and Learning in Regional Australia

Fukuyama, F, 1995. *Trust: The Social Virtues and the Creation of Prosperity*. New York: The Free Press

Health Development Agency, 2000. *Art for Health: a review of good practice in community-based arts projects and initiatives, which impact on health and well-being*. London: HAD

Hill, R, & Moriarty, G, 2001... as broadcast in Beijing. *Merseyside ACME. A Social Impact Study*. Merseyside: ACME

Home Office, 1999. *Report of the Policy Action Team 9, Community Self-Help*, Active Community Unit, Home Office

Housing Corporation, (2003) *Involvement Policy For the Housing Association Sector*, Housing Corporation

Institute for Employment Research, 2001. *Projections of Occupations and Qualifications: 2000/2001: Research in support of the National Skills Task Force:* Department for Education and Employment

Joseph Rowntree Foundation, 2001. *Findings: Poverty and Social Exclusion in Britain*. Available online at www.jrf.org.uk

Kelly, P. *Pride and Patronage,* Plymouth City Council

Landry, C, Greene, L, Matarasso, F, and Bianchini, F, 1996. *The Art of Regeneration: Urban Renewal Through Cultural Activity.* Stroud: Comedia

Lewis, B, 2000. *Housing % For Art: Conference Report 29th March 2000.* Pontefract Press

LGA, 2001. *Realising the Potential of Cultural Services: The Case for the Arts.* Research Briefing Twelve Point Four, Local Government Association

Lingayah, S. MacGillvray, A. and Raynard, P, 1996. *Creative Accounting: Beyond the Bottom Line. The Social Impact of Arts Programmes*, Working Paper 2, Comedia

Matarasso, F, 1996. *Defining Values: Evaluating Arts Programmes, The Social Impact of the Arts, Working Paper 1*. Stroud. Comedia

Matarasso, F, 1997. *Use or Ornament? The Social Impact of Participation in the Arts.* Comedia

Moriarty, G, 1998. *Hidden Assets: The Role of Arts in Regeneration*. Bolton: Bolton Libraries Arts and Archives

Moriarty, G, McManus K, 2003. *Releasing the Potential: Creativity and Change.* Arts Council

Myerscough, J. Bruce, A, Feist A, Manton, K, Towse, R, and Vaughan, D, 1988. *The Economic Importance of the Arts in Britain*, London, Policy Studies Institute

Oatley, N, 1998. *Cities, Economic Competition and Urban Policy*, Paul Chapman Publishing Limited

P & R Policy & Research, 2000: *Revitalising Rekendyke*

Portes, A, Landolt P. 1996. *The Downside of Social Capital.* The American Prospect. May/June

Putnam, R, 1993. *Making Democracy Work: Civic Traditions in Modern Italy*, Princeton

Putnam, R, 1996. *The Strange Disappearance of Civic America*. American Prospect, Volume 7, Issue 24, December 1, 1996

Putnam, R, 2000. *Bowling Alone: The Collapse and Revival of American Community*. Simon and Schuster

Reeves, M 2002. *Measuring the Economic and Social Impact of the Arts. A Review.* Arts Council

Shah, A 2003. *What Works: Positive Activities for Young People*. Unpublished

Shaw, P, 1999. *The Arts and Neighbourhood Renewal, a literature review to inform the work of Policy Action Team 10*, DCMS

Shaw, P, 2003. *The Contribution of the Arts Programme of Look Ahead Housing and Care to the fulfillment of the organisationís strategic objectives.*

Shudson, M, 1996. *Unsolved Mysteries: The Tocqueville Files; What if civic life didnít die?* The American Prospect. Volume 7, Issue 25, March 1, 1996

The Unit for the Arts and Offenders, 2003. *Arts in Criminal Justice Settings: Research and Evaluation*

Williams, D, 1997. *How the Arts Measures up: Australian Research into the Social Impact of the Arts, The Social Impact of the Arts*, Working Paper 8. Stroud: Comedia

World Bank , 2002. *What is Social Capital?* From www.worldbank.org/poverty/scapital

133

Useful websites

www.designcouncil.org.uk/design/content/publication
'*What learning needs: The challenge for a creative nation*'
A Design Council/Demos report on the role of creativity in education, June 2001

*"We planned the project
and community involvement
came with it."*

Trevor Evans, Got What it Takes

www.dfes.gov.uk/naccce
All our futures: Creativity, culture and education
A report by the National Advisory Committee on
Creative and Cultural Education (NACCCE) to the
Secretaries of State for Education and Employment
and Culture, Media and Sport, 1999.

www.ncaction.org.uk/creativity/creativity_report.pdf
*Analysis of research and literature on creativity in
education*
A report prepared for QCA by Anna Craft, March
2001

www.inca.org.uk/thematic.asp
*The arts, creativity and cultural education: An
international perspective*
A report in the series of thematic studies, published
as part of the International Review of Curriculum
and Assessment Frameworks project. Carried out
by the National Foundation for Educational
Research in England and Wales (NFER) on
behalf of QCA.

www.designcouncil.org.uk/design/content/publication
Changing behaviours
A series of essays by leading thinkers, introduced by
Design Council chairman Christopher Frayling. These
contribute to the debate about the role of education
in harnessing and encouraging creativity, examine the
latest research and look at examples of creativity in
action. They explore the potential for mutual benefit
in partnerships between universities, colleges and
businesses, and consider the effects that physical
environments can have on creativity.

www.capeuk.org
Creative Arts Partnerships in Education
A long-term action research project set up in 1997. It
involves schools in the Leeds and Manchester
conurbations seeking new ways of approaching the
curriculum through innovation and creativity. It was
inspired by an innovative arts education project in
Chicago where learning, motivation, achievement
and drop-out rates were significantly improved
among the young people taking part.